ONCE IN NAM, ALWAYS IN NAM

ONCE IN NAM, ALWAYS IN NAM

Richard T. Edwards

The New Atlantian Library

The New Atlantian Library
is an imprint of
ABSOLUTELY AMAZING eBOOKS

Published by Whiz Bang LLC, 926 Truman Avenue, Key West, Florida 33040, USA.

Once in Nam, Always in Nam copyright © 2018 by Richard T. Edwards. Electronic compilation / paperback edition copyright © 2018 by Whiz Bang LLC.

All rights reserved. No part of this book may be reproduced, scanned, or transmitted in any form or by any means, electronic or mechanical, including photocopying, recording, or any information storage and retrieval system, without permission in writing from the publisher. Please do not participate in or encourage piracy of copyrighted materials in violation of the author's rights. Purchase only authorized ebook editions.

This work is based on factual events. While the author has made every effort to provide accurate information at the time of publication, neither the publisher nor the author assumes any responsibility for errors, or for changes that occur after publication. Further, the publisher does not have any control over and does not assume any responsibility for author or third-party websites or their contents. How the e-book displays on a given reader is beyond the publisher's control.

For information contact
Publisher@AbsolutelyAmazingEbooks.com
ISBN-13: 978-1945772832 (The New Atlantian Library)
ISBN-10: 1945772832

ONCE IN NAM, ALWAYS IN NAM

FORWARD

IF YOU GOT IN YOUR CAR today and went for a drive but never came back, how far would you go?

What would you see?

What would you remember?

What if you knew you could never go back home?

What if you crashed into another car and watched while the occupants in the other car including kids burn alive while you couldn't move to save them?

A horrific thought, right?

Well, that pretty much sums up all the mental anguish, trauma and misery many Vietnam Veterans face. But they are not alone. They are the old people these days. There are even younger Veterans. But this time, they aren't just men, there are women who have experienced the horrors of war.

There stories are no more different than the ones we had faced in the past. Just as horrible, just as bloody and just as wrong.

The biggest difference, thanks to some of us Veterans, they are better trained and briefed on what their mission is, have a much better discipline system and, basically, don't get thrown into the deep end of a pool and get told sink or swim.

Some just sunk and without life preservers, died.

If I could point my finger at one specific reason why we lost so many good men in Vietnam, my target would be the lack of understanding by the public of what the term GI means. Which is, you are a slave to a bunch of over rated boy scouts who own none of the responsibilities for getting their soldiers killed or mentally or physically maimed because the GI is a replaceable statistic on someone's spreadsheet. After all, it is the responsibility of the top brass whose career is on the line if they don't get the job done.

In their wake for upward mobility, a sad but fact, the brass sits back in a war room and assesses the mission assignment based on accomplishment rather than on how not to put their subordinate men and woman in harm's way.

The second biggest mistake was the belief that the Vietnam War was a conventional gentleman's war. Perhaps, we forgot we didn't win the Revolutionary War going head to head against a well-trained Red Coats. We were the ones who had the home team advantage and guerilla warfare tactics seemed to work fine for us, as well.

The third biggest mistake we made in Vietnam was radio chatter. We may have air superiority in Vietnam, but we didn't when it came to the use of radio to communicate our activities, we compromised every move we made using our radios.

This couldn't be more obvious when we evacuated Firebase Ripcord.

Many soldiers died – I believe over half of our causalities – because we depended on radios to call in supplies, equipment and grid coordinates via PRC-77 radios and the like to get our jobs done. And let's be clear about this, our enemy had plenty of time to learn how to use our radios against us. And, because most of the actions were being called in from the Pentagon, so did our enemy at home.

The fourth biggest mistake was not briefing the soldiers why they were important to the success or failure of their units. I know this is hard to believe but if you asked an E-5 or below what his mission was in Vietnam, you would get a blank look. And then probably hear, "Whatever they tell me to do, sir." Not "Our mission is to support our infantry soldiers with close quarters aerial rocker artillery support, sir".

The fifth biggest mistake was allowing the press corps to do anything they damn well wanted to do. And let's face it, when their goal is to take pictures of and write stories about all the bad things that were going to sell their work and win the Pulitzer, you don't exactly get a balanced picture on what was really going on.

This was fixed by the time Desert Storm came along because the centralization of Public Affairs was realigned by me to enable unit level – what was once called stringers – to control what the press corps could cover and where they could go. (Who says a lonely E-5 can't have significant impact on the Army?)

The last biggest mistake we made was with the Army's inability to enable recognizable resources and apply their skills and talents. There was way too much emphasis on recognition of what the officers did and way too little recognition of the decisive actions that many of the younger enlisted played on the outcome of events that, without their heroics, many bad situations would have been much worse and not turned out to be better.

I have a retired LTG by the name of John N. Brandenburg, whom at the time was Command Officer of the 101st Airborne Division Air Assault who knows and has recognized exactly what that means. There's a letter of appreciation in my files from him reflecting that understanding.

We have had our days to say the least.

So, why, exactly, am I adding to the pile of books on Vietnam? Because my belief is that there is still a body of work that needs to be written about our unique unit and the men – and women – who made living in the hell of Vietnam bearable and one soldier can make a difference if he can do so.

I also believe that you are going to find that not all

Once in Nam, Always in Nam

of us Vietnam Veterans paint their stories the same way. And by that, I mean, some of us came home with a more mature outlook on life while others just never left. Hence the name of the book: What happened in Nam stays in Nam.

- Richard T. Edwards

CONTENTS

WHAT THE HELL DID I JUST DO
BASIC TRAINING
ADVANCED INDIVIDUAL TRAINING
AH-1G COBRA OVERVIEW
HOW WE BALANCED ROTOR BLADES WITH DUCT TAPE
WHAT, EXCATLY, WAS THE 4th BATTALION, 77th FIELD ARTILLERY
HEADING FOR VIETNAM
WELCOME TO VIETNAM
SERTS TRAINING AND CALL HIM SIR
THE NIGHT I SALUTED SANTA
HEADING FOR CAMP EAGLE
GOING TO THE TRUCK WASH
REBUILDING A COBRA Part 1
REBUILDING A COBRA Part 2
REBUILDING A COBRA Part 3
REASSIGNED TO B BATTERY, 4/77th FIELD ARTILLERY (ARA)
GETTING IN AIR TIME FOR AN AIR MEDAL
THOSE PUSH PULL BEARINGS IN MY BUDDY'S POCKET SAVE THE DAY
EXPO 70
HEADING BACK FROM SIGON
COMMAND AND CONTROL NORTH
FIREBASE RIPCORD
SO WHY ARE YOU WHISPERING?
HEADED TO EAGLE BEACH
THE NIGHT I WATCHED 5 SOLDIERS DIE
WHERE'S THE PAPER CLIPS
DAY I WENT TO LAW SCHOOL
HEADING TO THE HOSPITAL SHIP SANCTUARY

HERE'S A LITTLE CS IN YOUR FACE
HEADING BACK TO OSAKA TO MEET THE 5TH
  DIMENSON
GOING UP TO THE DMZ
THE NIGHT MASH GOT TRASHED
BATES GETS CORT MARTIALED
RICHARD NIXON TOOK AWAY MY GTO
INCOMING IN AND INCOMING OUT
COMING HOME
LOOKING BACK THROUGH THE EYES OF
  A 68-YEAR-OLD
STUFF THAT JUST DOESN'T FIT ELSEWHERE
THE BREAKFAST CLUB
WARRANT OFFICER FRED CAPPO
STARLIGHT, STAR BRIGHT, TELL ME THERE
  AIN'T NO CHARLIE CONG IN MY
    WIRES TONIGHT
MUD, MUD, GLORIOUS MUD
THE DAY MEN WERE OVERCOME BY A FORCE
  THAT WON THEIR HEARTS
I AM USELESS WITHOUT MY P-38
C-RATIONS SOCIALIZATION IN A BOX
FSANGC RAIDS
FICTION AND BITS & PIECES OF FICTION
ROLL ON BROTHER, ROLL ON
A HELL OF A STORY
MAIL CALL
ICE CREAM TRUCKS WEAPONS OF
  MASS DESTRUCTION
YOU HAD TO DIE TO GET BETTER

WHAT THE HELL DID I JUST DO?

BACK IN MY TIME, 1969, there were three ways you could be on active duty. You were drafted -US, you volunteered –RA, you were on active duty as a National Guard -NG or you were on active duty as a Reservist- USAR.

The idea here was that if you volunteered for active duty, you could pick and choose what job you wanted in the military if you signed on the dotted line for 3 or more years and not the 2 the drafted soldiers were obligated to serve.

As it turned out, it was all BS because once you signed up as an enlisted, the Army really didn't have to keep its part of the bargain. Which would have been fine provided that the goal was to send you to Vietnam.

Bear in mind that my father was a recruiter in the 1950s. So, he could have easily told me the truth about the reality of signing up for three years. He even came with me while the recruiter was providing me with a job description. And assured that what I was signing up for was going to be the job I would get.

I may have well had the devil himself beside me when I did sign up. Because the contract said CMF or Career Management Force. And what that meant was I had no control over what CMF needed at the time I signed up.

Of course, I didn't know any of this at first. All I knew is that I signed up to be a fixed wing aircraft mechanic and that's what I really wanted to do. But again, what you want to do and what the Army wants to do with you –since once you sign on the dotted line

– are two different things.

After signing up, I headed to Newark, NJ for a physical. After being in your shorts for 3 hours, if you have the right scores, the Army Security Agency wants to talk to you about adding an additional year to your contract.

Who in their right mind would want to sign up for an additional year when you hear, "I can't tell you what you'll be doing but if you sign up for an additional year, you can join up with the ASA."

Like, really, are you kidding?

After that, you go into a room where you raise your hand and repeat the usual chant one does upon initial enlistment and every time one re-enlists. I suppose you're supposed to take it seriously. But in all honesty, unless everyone in the United States read it, they would be quick to realize just how powerful the President of the United States is.

"I, your name, do solemnly swear (or affirm) that I will support and defend the Constitution of the United States against all enemies, foreign and domestic; that I will bear true faith and allegiance to the same; and that I will obey the orders of the President of the United States and the orders of the officers appointed over me, according to regulations and the Uniform Code of Military Justice. So, help me God." both foreign and domestic."

The kicker here is that no one in the room ever asks to read the Uniform Code of Military Justice (UMDMJ). I honestly believe if they did, they would never sign up for the Military.

The UCMJ is federal law, enacted by Congress. The UCMJ defines the military justice system and lists criminal offenses under military law.

The law requires the President of the United States, acting as commander-in-chief of the Armed Forces, to write rules and regulations to implement military law. The President writes these rules and regulations by issuing an executive order known as the *Manual for Courts-Martial* (MCM). The MCM details rules and regulations for military court-martials and provides for maximum punishments for each military offense listed in the punitive articles of the UCMJ.

Also, "and the orders of the officers appointed over me." That line just gets to me. Because when you're new to this military game, your idea as to what an officer has probably been tainted by TV shows, what you've read and what you think you know what officer is.

An officer can be an Officer, Warrant Officer, and a Non-Commissioned Officer.

An officer - 01 through O10 – can be an officer from West Point, OCS, and ROTC. In times of war, an enlisted can become an Officer but these are rare.

A Warrant Officer is an officer that is either so highly technical his or her area of expertise that that Army wants to keep him or her in the military or has been trained by the military – such as a pilot.

A Non-commissioned Officer is anyone above the rank of E-4 with hard stripes. Meaning, if you are an E-3 or below, everyone above you can pretty much make your life miserable. Most enlisted men and woman reach E-3 within 90 days of being in service and if they go to Advanced Individual Training (AIT) can go from E-4 to E-6 upon completion of their training.

Welcome to the wonderful world of the US Army!

THE BASICS OF BASIC TRAINING

BEING A MILITARY BRAT, you pretty much know what to expect from basic training. Especially, when your dad used to wear that Smokey The Bear hat. The gist of it is, basic training is designed to make you feel like they are whipping you into shape both mentally and physical to do exactly what the Army wants you to do no questions asked.

The problem is, you are most likely out of shape, – which I wasn't even though I knew better, I wasn't – you're going to hear lot of drop and give me 20 on your first day and that probably won't stop for days on end.

Your hair on your head is going away, your days of freedom are gone for at least half the time you are in basic training. But as far as I'm concerned, this will be the best 8 to 12 weeks of your life in the military.

Why?

Because, it becomes personal. You've got to want to get in shape.

Want proof?

When you go to the mess hall – and believe me, you're going to be going to the mess hall to eat and probably do some kitchen police (KP) duty as well – you have an option to eat the food and not lose much weight or not eat the food and, get in shape.

I chose to get in shape and I went from 200 pounds of flubber to 185 pounds and you could see the abs. Also, I challenged myself on those areas of the PT test I was weakest at. The result from the fitness point of view was a promotion to E-2 out of basic training.

But there was more. While it kicked like a mule, the

Once in Nam, Always in Nam

M-14, with its .308 caliber rounds, and I got pretty good at hitting targets. Especially, the one that was 450 yards out. And after learning how to use that weapon, the M-16 was a tinker toy.

Nevertheless, I scored Sharpshooter on the M-14 and Marksman on the M-16.

How many people can say that had an M-60 machine gun fired over their heads, crawled under barbed wire and went through an obstacle course like there's nothing to it?

See what I mean about it all being an individual effort?

That's really what it's all about.

My best memory was beating the crap out of a 6'5" National Guard solider with a bungee stick. I pretended it was Franko Harris who played football for Mount Holly and just plaster the guy with a volley of smashes and bashes until he was on the ground begging for mercy.

Okay, I just made that up. The Franco Harris.

I don't think the NG guy could do anything but defend himself from my onslaught. Still, it made me feel good. Really good.

The only embarrassing moment I had was when I called my rifle a gun and I had to run around the solders saying, "This is my rifle, and this is my gun. This is for shooting and this is for fun."

We also had some very colorful cadre. One, obviously from the Deep South used to tell us, "Ain't no way you pathetic slugs are coming home alive from Vietnam. You'll be wearing body bag instead of a uniform. Move you're your sorry asses. MOVE!"

Or, "You boys are in for a world of hurt!"

And closer to the end of our time: "Yellow River. River of Saigon. Yellow River, one more river to cross."

It was something we all felt we were going to

understand more about in the near and distant future.

After getting promoted and going through the usual ceremony drill of passing Basic Training, we were given orders. Mine looked wrong.

So, I asked one of the Drill Instructors (DIs) what it meant, and he was brutally honest with me, "It means, solider, that you're going to Vietnam."

Then he said, "It also means you're going to be working with the AH-1G Cobra helicopter, the most advanced attack helicopter in the world."

ADVANCED INDIVIDUAL TRAINING

OR AIT FOR SHORT. There are so many of these that I could write a book on all of them. The only one I want to cover here is the one that I had to take – with a mixed bag of attitude.

The general mechanics course included training on the different nuts and bolts used, the different gauges of safety wire and how many turns per inch are acceptable, the various tools used with working on an aircraft. Basic hydraulics, working with aircraft tubing, reading electrical schematics, the assortment of technical manuals used the various kinds of safety wire and how to use the safety wire pliers, the different types of nuts and bolts used and naming conventions such as Zeus fasteners, lock nuts and carter pins.

Actual hands on training included working with 1/4-inch metal sheets, bending them, drilling holes in them and the use of rivets. Included was the use of cherry lock rivet gun with cherry locked rivets.

Power plant and drive train assemblies were also part of the training. Cross sectional cuts of turbines were shown and terms such as stator and rotor blades became test questions along with the various stages the inside a turbine engine.

A passing score in this phase earned you E-3.

All this general enough to be applied to any aircraft mechanic's job.

AH-1G COBRA OVERVIEW

WHEN I FIRST SAW one of these beasts of a machine, I figured I had to be a masochist, because I fell in love with it. The AG-1H Cobra Helicopter is a beast. It stands 13 feet high, is 36 inches wide, and is around 47 feet long. It has dual hydraulics, dual controls, a turret and wing stores on both sides of the helicopter.

It also had a different kind of stabilizing system known as the 540-rotor head system. Meaning there was no stabilizer bar. Instead, pressure sensitive resistance indicators detected the differences in yaw, pitch and roll which sent this information to a SCAS box which sat behind the pilot which caused gyros to electronically react to the differences and then send auto corrections to the hydraulic actuators to automatically adjust to the changes.

The result is one smoothest flying machines in the world at that time.

From front to back, there was something that could break. The pitot tube, the battery compartment – which proved to be a weight and balance issue and was moved to a rear compartment – was used by crew chiefs to store Plexiglas cleaner and wipes to the stinger section. If it moved or was on the Cobra, it could become a maintenance issue

The pilots sat in tandem. The pilot in the back seat. The gunner in the front seat

The Cobra provided the pilots with a very wide view – above 270 degrees – of the situation below them. The hydraulic reservoirs were located just past the Plexiglas canopy and the back seat. It was made from magnesium and while the system itself was under 3,000 psi, these reservoirs simply acted as a place where the levels were checked, and the fluid simply flowed through them.

Anyway, names such as power plant, short shaft, transmission, swash plate, scissors and sleeve assembly, lollypops, main rotor blades and Jesus nut were what went from the airframe to the rotor blades. Also, from the transmission came the hanger bearings, rotor shafts, 42-degree gearbox, 90-degree gearbox, tail rotor assembly and push-pull bearings.

Giving you a headache yet. I don't get headaches and that's enough to give anyone one.

Imagine all the wiring, all the other tubes and systems involved inside the framework of body of this flying machine, and you have a good idea as what I had to learn to pass the Cobra mechanic's course.

I almost didn't thanks to a guy by the name of Bates who stole my red and black pencil and left me with only a black led pencil because he was pissed off I wouldn't cheat for him. I had an 87-score going into the last test. Thanks to Bates, without a red pencil, I couldn't correctly answer four questions.

You'll hear more about him later.

I also tried to go to Airborne School. I worked just as hard on learning as much as I could on the Cobra as I did, in passing the rigorous physical test to qualify for Airborne School.

But when it came to the physical the doctor said, "Young man, there are two reasons why I can't qualify you for Airborne School, you have no depth perception and you are already on orders for Vietnam."

Well, hell, I suppose I should be worried about walking right up to the main rotor blade or tail rotor, since I supposedly don't know how far that was either. Didn't I just flag a 310 RPM main rotor blade for check and balance?

I think someone is overusing the word depth perception for the words binocular vision.

HOW WE BALANCED ROTOR BLADES WITH DUCT TAPE

USING DUCT TAPE to align rotor blades? Sound farfetched? Not at all. In fact, it's common.

Technically speaking, this procedure can occur almost anywhere in the world and at any time; not specifically novel to Vietnam.

From a mechanic's perspective, it is one of the most dangerous part of the job. Here's the procedure:

First, you mark the edge of the blade where the securing hook goes – a piece of metal about a 1/4 of an inch thick – with one side blue and the other side red.

A pilot gets in the back seat and starts up the helicopter. With the blades turning at 320 rpm above your head, you walk up under them, figure out where the end tip of the blades is, and mark it with your boot.

A flag is used. This is a metal pole that has a handle at waist level and two pieces of metal sticking out from the center pole at 90 degrees to the handle. Between those two pieces of metal, are two pieces of rope. Wrapped around the rope is tape. This tape is what the blades will strike.

So, the first time this procedure is done, the pilot adjusts the blades, so they will hit the tape and not the metal pole. The job of the mechanic at that point is to bring the pole up a few inches away from the turning blades and then turn the pole so the tape gets hit by the turning blades.

Once this happens, the helicopter is shut down, the lower blade's buckshot cap is opened and inspected for steel balls. Six sills move the blade up a half-inch. But there is 3/4 of an inch more to get the alignment correct – perhaps.

For a second time, the pilot adjusts the blades, so they will hit the tape and not the metal pole. With fresh tape added, the blade strikes the tape. Now, there's only a half-inch difference between the lower red and the higher blue.

This time, duct tape is applied to the blue blade near the trailing edge of it. Two complete turns of the tape. Each wrap representing 3 steel balls.

This should bring it below the red line. We test to see. Got through the procedures and sure enough, just a little below the red line.

Tape comes off and 4 steel balls are added to the blue blade's buckshot cap.

After new tape is added to the flag, the pilot starts up the cobra and we bring the flag into the spinning blades. The two marks are right on top of each other/. The buckshot caps tightened down as per specifications, get safety wired and approved by the technical inspector.

That's pretty much how we used duct tape to balance rotor blades.

WHAT, EXACTLY, WAS THE 4ᵀᴴ BATTALION, 77ᵀᴴ FIELD ARTILLERY

IF THE 4077 was a M*A*S*H unit, then the 4/77th was a B*A*S*H unit. A Battalion of Assault Helicopters — 36 AH IG Cobras to be precise.

The one thing you're going to notice about this book is, aside from here, there is no clear description of what is the 4th Battalion, 77th Field Artillery.

That's because none of knew was it was or how significant the unit was with respect to its role in supporting ground forces with close quarters artillery support.

The 4th Battalion, 77th Field Artillery (Aerial Rocket Artillery) consisted of A Battery-Dragons, B Battery – El Toros and C Battery – Griffins. There was also the headquarters Company.

Anyway, each of the three Batteries had 12 AH-IG Cobras assigned to them and each was in a key location: A Battery, in Phu Bai, B Battery, at Camp Eagle and C Battery, at Camp Evans. And each had an arrow painted between the wing stores and the stabilizer. A Battery had a red arrow, B Battery had a white arrow and C Battery had a blue arrow.

Each Battery was broken down into sections. A 2-minute, 5-minute, 15 minutes and a standby section. What this meant, was when a Fire Mission was called, the 2-minute section would be called and within 2 minutes they would be airborne, and the 5-minute section would become the new 2-minute section and so forth and so on.

Before going into an example of a fire mission, what we brought to the friendly forces for close quarter support as far as firepower is concerned is key to understanding just how important the power of the arsenal was to the solders needing it.

THE TURRET

The turret can have two mini guns, or two 40mm grenade launchers or 1 of each. The Cobra's front sear had a hand-held gunner sight system that turned the turret as he tracked a target in the center of his sight. Both pilots could fire the turret, the back seat would only be able to fire it in the in the straight position as he could be using his fixed sight for both wing stores and turret.

Specific pairs of rockets could be selected by the back seat.

THE WING STORES

The aircraft could carry seventy-two 2.75-inch folding fin aerial rockets with a 10-pound warhead.

A combination of 17-pound rockets with 10-pound rockets was also possible but it also meant that for every two 17-pounders, you would have to drop 2 10-pound rockets. So, if you wanted 36 17-pounders, you could carry 18 10-pounders. Or a total of 54 rockets.

We had four types of rockets we used.

White Phosphorus rocket that was used to mark targets.

High explosive rockets (HE) were rounds that were used to destroy vehicles, bunkers, knock down trees, shoot boats, and hit troops dug in.

Variable time fuse rockets (VT) were used to shoot troops in the open. The fuse of the rocket sent out a signal and would explode exactly 20 feet above the ground. It was difficult to hide from this one and it covered a large area on the ground with shrapnel.

Flachette rockets (Nails) had a warhead with 5,000 little darts (nails) inside. They would detonate in the air above the target and a single pair could cover every square foot of a football field.

They were great for troops hiding in tall grass or in trees. Infantry troops on the ground would often report enemy soldiers literally nailed to a tree or the ground. (Courtesy of Lt. Craig Gies.)

Now, let's go on a fire mission.

FIRE MISSION!

AH-IG Cobra configuration we used weren't called "heavy hogs" for nothing. Even with less fuel compensating for 36 17-pound and 36 10-pound rockets, you just didn't pull pitch, hover at 10 feet, lower the nose and you were on the way.

These Cobras had to build momentum.

So, the pilot in each Cobra would pick up a few feet off the tarmac and gently noised forward. For almost 100 feet, the Cobras would pick up speed and went on their way.

Inside the cockpit, the back seat received grid coordinates from Division Artillery (DIV ARTY), in cryptic formant. Both pilot and co-pilot wore an Encryption Decoder. Each day was a tear out and throw away page and the CEOI was replaced monthly.

Once grid coordinates were confirmed, they were written on the Plexiglas and the pilot flew to that location to contact the friendly forces requesting support.

While all of this is going on between the pilots and establishing the objective, the front seat, made sure all the armament systems were technically operational. This included his sighting system.

Because of the 180-degree visual view of the

situation, once over the target, the lead Cobra pilot would assess the best direction and angle to best support the friendly forces on the ground.

The Cobras were generally flown in a circular pattern. They started their "run" at 3000 feet and would first use a set of white phosphorous rounds to mark the target and assure accuracy and placement of the rockets.

As the one Cobra had completed its run and was at its most vulnerable position – recovering from the dive and gaining altitude, the other Cobra was protecting it with its run against the target.

If the two-minute section thought additional support was needed to get the job done, the PC or Pilot in Command could elect to call in another section or ask for additional air support.

This generally came in the form of F-4 Phantoms from Da Nang.

With another section on station, the 2-minute section would come back in, get refueled and rearmed. If the 5 and 15-minute sections couldn't handle the rest of the mission by themselves, then the standby section would be launched.

After refueling and rearming, the two-minute section would generally hover over to their launching area and shut down.

When everything went well, there were lots of smiles and crew chiefs were patted on the back for making the mechanic portion of the air to ground experience flawless.

When things went bad, logbooks noted the issues, and everyone jumped in to make sure it didn't happen again.

I've seen times when the 2-minute section didn't launch for days. I've also seen times when they launched three times in one day.

Richard T. Edwards

HEADING FOR VIETNAM

WE WERE AT THE GARDNER MANSION and I was saying goodbye to my best friend Julie.

"Aren't you scared," she asked.

"Of course, I am," I admitted. "I wouldn't be human if I wasn't. But I am on orders so, I don't have much of a choice."

"Well, will you write to me?" she began pouting.

"Of course, I will. Just give me your address on a piece of paper."

As tears rolled down her face, she wrote down her address and handed to me.

"You don't write to me and I will kill you," she said in a teasing manner.

"Julie, I will be back."

We hugged, and I kissed her on her cheek. I headed for the door. "Thanks Mr. and Mrs. Gardner, for everything."

I didn't wait for an answer. I just closed the door behind me. And felt the weight of the world lighten up on my shoulders. I never did write to Julie. Not because I didn't want to. But because her life of living in a mansion was too much competition for me on a poor boy's income. Especially one with a $90 per month income for the next 2 years and 6 months.

What type of life could I provide her? I was on the wrong side of the tracks. And she should have the best of her world. And even at $80 per week from Addressograph\Multigraph and working a side line job when I got back home, it still wouldn't size up to a Mansion. So, it was, I opened the door or warmth and welcome and closed it. On the other side was cold and loneliness.

That was the way it had to be. That's the way it was.

I was a PFC. And I was scared. Other than Basic and AIT, I've never been too far away from home.

Combine that with the fact that you're headed for Vietnam where in less than five minutes after you hit Charlie Country, you could be going back home in a body bag. Yeah, you're going to want to score a few times before you go.

Well, that didn't happen for me. My mother had other plans for me and we spent some quality times together. Even my father wanted to say good-bye before I left.

Come to think of it, I think everyone I knew took their turn to drop by and wanted to say good-bye and good luck.

Did they know something I didn't know? I have a good imagination. So, these guys in a dark black room with a light shining on a beer stained green felt Black Jack smoking their stogies:

"Okay, Edwards. 100 to 1 says he's in a body bag five minutes after he land in Vietnam."

"1000 to 1 says he's KIA."

Meanwhile, a tall white-haired stranger with beautiful blue eyes walks up to the table, sits down and says. "365 to 1 says he's coming back in 1 piece."

"And who the hell are you?"

"His guardian angel."

On the night before I left to head back over to Fort Dix, while I was drinking all the sounds and fond memories I had in Moorestown, NJ, the one thing I loved to do the most made its presence clear. The sound of a far-away passenger train coming in from Camden, NJ and heading for Mount Holly, NJ.

A whispering force of man-made hell. A dynamic daemon of destiny following it. Floating above and through time.

Once in Nam, Always in Nam

Reminding me of that old lady on Stanwick and 3rd waving and crying while GIs on their train of destiny.

One that none on that express train to Fort Dix would know was inevitable and just as predictable as their names in the obituary column.

Scribed by the hand of death himself.

It was just a matter of time, place and circumstance. A spectacular horror Steven King would have trouble writing and describing on paper.

You would have to be on that train to destiny, feel the bullet hit you head, your chest or the mortar round blow up in front of your face to know the true horror of war.

When you are so close to those screams from the men bleeding out and then come back to the States with such blood curling memories, I'm pretty sure the last thing on your mind is to want to talk about it like its front-page news.

Vietnam was the front-page headlines from hell.

All take all the angel support I could get.

I got up the next morning, did the usual three S's, ate breakfast, packed my duffle bag, kissed my mom, got in the car with my dad and we headed over to Fort Dix, NJ. My mother's tears fading softly in my mind as we got closer to Fort Dix.

"Son, I'm proud of you," he said. He shook my hand. I got out pulled my duffle from out of the back seat.

"Goodbye, dad." I said as I closed the door. And then stood there watching the tail lights fading into the dusk.

"Hey soldier, are you lost?"

That put a smile on my face. It was a friend of mine from AIT.

"Not as long as you're around," I said.

Richard T. Edwards

WELCOME TO VIETNAM

OF ALL THE PEOPLE on the 707 landing at Long Bin in November 1969, I think the most edgy were those who had already served there. They know what we couldn't know. Some of us on that plane were not going to come back and many would be either physically or mentally wounded or both.

For me, the flight started from Fort Dix, New Jersey on a chartered civilian airliner. And had two more stops before touching down in Vietnam. While many were still drunk, we landed in Fairbanks, Alaska and then at Yokota Air Base for fuel. But all the while on the flight many of us focused on the female flight attendants. Perhaps the last chance in our lives to breathe in the sweet scents, enjoy the beauty or hear the voice of an American female.

Camh Ranh Bay was an image of white pillars of smoke – burning human waste as we learned later, dusty sky and a bee hive of all sorts of flying machines which seemed to pop out of nowhere and disappeared just as quickly as they were scene. When the doors opened, hot humid air filled your lungs.

The smell of kerosene, rockets, and axle grease toyed with your nostrils. The screams of turbines coupled with the pounding of rotor blades broken only by the 2-and-a-half-ton flatbed trucks known as duce and a half did nothing to silence the roaring voice of the man moving us into a metal building where we were told where we were going next.

Our next stop was Bien Hoa. This is where the Screaming Eagle Replacement Training Section (SERTS) was located and where the first physical reminder of hell on earth stood out. Burnt plywood decorated with shrapnel didn't need a voice to tell that story.

I'm sure the soldier killed there had little vocal cords left anyway.

The boom box near the corner of the building played the "Beatles Come Together":

Here comes old flattop he come grooving up slowly
  He got joo-joo eyeball he one holy roller
  He got hair down to his knee
  Got to be a joker he just does what he please
  He wears no shoeshine he got toe-jam football
  He got monkey finger he shoots Coca-Cola
  He says "I know you, you know me"
  One thing I can tell you is you got to be free
  Come together right now over me
  He bass' production he got walrus gumboot
  He got Ono sideboard he one spinal cracker
  He got feet down below his knee
  Hold you in his armchair you can feel his disease
  Come together right now over me
  He rollercoaster he got early warning
  He got muddy water he one mojo filter
  He says "One and one and one is three"
  Got to be good-looking 'cause he's so hard to see
  Come together right now over me

You know, as much as I hate the Beatles, for some reason this song was probably the most appropriate one for that moment in my life. And it felt good.

We sat down and some tall, lanky, spit shine Mississippi E7 dude with a mean ass looking baseball hat walked in and the room got deadly quiet.

"Men," he began, "Welcome to Vietnam. My name is Sergeant Perfect, and I will oversee this group's in country processing. You will be mine for the next 10 days. You will be given your orders for the units you will be assigned to up north, you will be given your combat fatigues and your TA-50 gear, and you will be given a day off to overcome jet lag.

"You will then attend the Screaming Eagle Replacement Training School (SERTS). I don't care what your MOS is. Whether, you're a cook, an aircraft mechanic or a clerk in the orderly room, you're all going to be infantry solders for a week.

"You will all become familiar or more familiar with a variety of weapons…."

At the end of this 30-minute conversion:

"Most of you saw the holes in the plywood, the boom box with the Beatles Come Together on top of a duffle bag. Not my kind of music either.

"The holes in the plywood was where Charlie landed on of his mortars and killed one of you about a year ago. The war is around you. You are the front line.

"To prove my point," He pulls out a clacker and squeezes it. The sound of an M80 goes off and a cloud of white flour can be seen behind us.

"I just love doing that," he said with a matter of fact yet funny kind of way.

"Now listen up. Since I don't like boom boxes but don't plan on replacing it every two weeks, you all didn't get the satisfaction of seeing the Beatles and the boom box being thrown into the air and then being smashed into pieces.

"But imagine that was you. At best, you just lost a body part and I'm sure there's at least one you don't want to live without.

"What if that was you?

"Stop and think, men, before you act. Instinctive reactions may save your life when you are in the heat of the battle, but they can kill you when you aren't.

"The goal of SERTS training is to provide you with

80 hours of additional in country training designed to increase your chances of survival no matter where you work, no matter what job title you have.

"Unfortunately, some of you will receive wounds from bullets and shrapnel. Some of you will be missing body parts.

"Some of you will die.

"Move out!"

The rest of the day was spent on the in-country processing, exchange of stateside fatigues to combat fatigues, the sowing of our names on them and hooch assignments and a quick user guide to where the mess hall was located. Which none of us used for an entire day.

I don't remember dreaming. Not of Julie Gardner. Not about her friendship that started up as kids. Or what I wanted to do with her in the back seat of my red 62 Chevy. I just remember the next morning wasn't the next morning.

It was Wednesday, day 3 in Vietnam and it was 6 am. Cold shower, teeth brushing, wearing combat fatigues for the first time and I'm headed for the mess hall.

As we walked through the door of the mess hall I was met by a pleasant surprise. It was the first time in my life that I saw not just a Warrant Officer a CW4 and one that looked like he had been in for 40 years. He had whitish silver hair.

Since no one was telling us what was going to happen next, I walked up to him, looked him dead in the eyes and said, "When, Sir".

After a few seconds, he spoke.

He said, "Tomorrow. You'll go to Bien Hoa, M-80s and trip wires. Watch your back."

"Thank you, Sir."

You start building fake friendships quickly so the

kid from New Hampshire asked, "So, what was that all about?"

"Wanted to know when SERTS training starts and he told me we're going tomorrow. He also said it won't be here but at Bien Hoa. They'll be waking us the next day with M-80s and to watch out for the trip wires."

"So, another does nothing day?"

"Actually two," I said.

"Boring," he countered.

Three buses of men who served their time in Nam passed me and the rest of the men heading for the mess hall and shouted out the words "look at all the cherries" or "hey cherry, go home and suck on your mama's tit."

The sounds continued along the processions of men walking to the mess hall and the buses passing us by, the aroma of booze mixing with marijuana and bus exhaust in the passing.

"Funny, isn't it? They were walking this same path one year prior," said a French flavored draw from behind me. That made me smile.

So, I turned around, "What's your MOS?"

"Sixty Seven November Twenty," he said, proudly, "You?"

"Sixty-Seven Yankee Twenty," where are you heading?

"A Company 5th Transportation Battalion."

"Really, so am I."

"Say you aren't planning on becoming a lifer, are you?"

"Hell no! Why did you ask?"

"RA on your duffle bag and the way you walk."

"The RA meant a fixed wing mechanic contract that never happened, and the walk means I'm an Army brat whose dad who marched us boys up the street for a crew cut. Both of which I am proud to say turned me into the poster child for the can't wait to get the hell out this man's Army association.

"I'm no more interested in the Army than you are."

"Good enough."

He would soon be calling me Jersey and I would be calling him Frenchie. It would be a friendship that would last if I were with A Company 5th Transportation Battalion. But I'm getting a bit ahead of myself.

SERTS TRAINING AND CALL HIM SIR

I WOULD LOVE to say that SERTS training held some fond memories. All I remember about that was them blowing M-80s under our asses if we fell asleep and the outside the perimeter excursion along a small muddy berm between rice paddies.

I volunteered to carry the radio.

Why not? No one else wanted the job.

Live to die. Enjoy the ride.

Speaking of rides, my best memory was hitching a ride with a short timer pilot who had 7 circled in back grease pencil the Plexiglas window of his slick. He was about to fly some ass and trash mission.

For all of us, our bodies had to adjust to the jet lag and the first day after arriving was pretty much uneventful as we slept that day into non-existence. The second day, we were marched over to the mess hall for morning breakfast.

We were paraded past busloads of troops heading home. All very anxious to leave. Some were wild with anticipation. Some drunk or high after smoking too much jungle weed. But a few looked scared as though it were all a joke. In their minds, the plane crashed before it took off and betting on the body bag. Two or three were still wearing bandages like a red badge of courage.

But all of them every one of them including the bus driver was very willing to let us know how much we were the "cherries".

Seriously, that's already getting old.

"Only half a class today," said Frenchie.

"Perhaps, for you," I argued, "I'm going for a walk. If anyone asks where I am, I took a dump."

15 minutes after lunch, I was over at the refueling point waiting for an UH-IH "Slick". One finally came in. This one had short timer written all over it.

You could tell the attitude of a short timer front seat every day of the week by his fast approach and skid-sliding landing. So, he is landing, and the crew chief jumped out and started working on filling up the chopper with the straw sweet smell of JP4. I approached the right side of the helicopter and asked if I could hitch a ride.

I also noticed 7 with a circle around it. He nodded his head and I moved back away until the refueling was done.

The crew chief walked up to me, pulled up his visor and said, "He told me to tell you to salute him the next time."

I walked up to the side of the helicopter where I was about to jump in and returned the salute I should have done previously. Got in, sat in the middle of the seat just behind the transmission bulkhead and buckled the seat belt around my waist.

The crew chief pushed up his mike and yelled, "The Captain wants to know if you need to get dropped back off here."

"Tell the Captain, yes Sir. And thank you."

The slick hovered a bit, backed out of the refueling point, turned and headed back the way it came.

All choppers have a story to tell. Bullet holes that have been patched up. Stuff like that. And this one was no different. Generally, they smell of JP4, hydraulic fluid and hot burnt charcoal. Some carry the smell of wounded soldiers. Others, the body odor smell of being scared shitless.

This one tingled the senses with a bit of all the

above.

Moments later we were at 100 feet in a tight turn around an unsuspecting duck about to be target practice for the door gunner. Watching the rounds hit around the duck, I figured he was either a bad aim or missing the fowl was on purpose.

Either way, after 25 rounds were fired we flew away and headed for a rubber plantation landing zone.

There, the signs of a real war hit home. There was a C-123 on the side of the strip with the farthest wing partially burned off. Burnt metal doesn't fly well. Temp buildings talked of being overrun and their contents blown to kingdom come. It was a sobering tapestry of war stories.

Right now, the C-4 rations needed to be off loaded. I went to volunteer to help move the boxes, but the crew chief motioned for me to stay put.

Five minutes later we were back in the air. The last part of my quick tour of Nam from the air brought us along a roadway where we followed a convoy of trucks ran into an ambush. We pulled pitch and climbed to a safe height. There was some quick scrambling for a terrain map.

The crew chief handed me a headset. And the pilot talked to me.

"These guys just came under attack. I'm going to call in some friendly air support. We have no business here and I have 21 days left. We need to get out of the way. We're taking you back to your pickup point."

I said "Yes, Sir. Thank you for letting me tag along, Sir."

He smiled.

By the time we turned and moved out of the target zone, two F-4s came screaming past. And for some reason at that moment and at that time, I felt good about being in Vietnam.

In less than an hour, I was back where I started from. I walked away from the chopper, turn, went into a formal posture and saluted the officers. And as I watched them once again fly out the way they came in, I did a little keep him safe for 21 days prayer.

I looked at my watch, 4:30 pm. I thought, I have plenty of time before the 5pm march over to the Mess Hall.

And I'm thinking. Wow, do I have a story to tell my newly found friend.

But then, I thought, nah, he wouldn't believe me anyway.

I recognized his shadowy frame waiting for me at the door.

"Where the hell have you been?"

"Why, did you miss me?

"No. So."

"So, you wouldn't believe me if I told you."

"Try me."

"Okay, over dinner. I've developed a bit of a hunger."

And off we went. The truth is, I saw more mental visual images on what was going on in one day than I saw the rest of my time in Vietnam.

Was it worth it? Hell, yes!

When you add this to the rest of what was left of the time spent in Bien Hoa with the stench of burning human waste and the scent of red clay dust, diesel fuel and JP4 you have the smell of hell's gate. I was at that gate eager to find out what was on the other side of it.

HEADING FOR CAMP EAGLE

SO, AFTER LEAVING LONG BINH and heading north for what seemed to be forever, we finally land at Phu Bai. Perhaps the most interesting feature of this landing strip is the traffic lights that are on Highway 1 on the north west side above the end of the runway and the south east side below the end of the runway. Both sets of lights turn red when an aircraft is on final on runway nine.

Phu Bai wasn't just an Air Force drop off point. I was also a base for both the Army and the Air Force. A hell in heaven and a heaven in hell.

Furthermore, there were much more AH-1G Cobras here than any place I have seen so far and a lot more of them in the air making their presence known with their distinctive main rotor blade sounds.

There was also a higher diversification of Army types on the ground. From infantry to logistical support, armor and artillery, warrant officers to Lieutenant Colonels.

Only problem is, being the monsoon season, you saluted everything with two feet coming at you because there was no way you could tell who in this soup was.

"Did we miss something in that briefing?" asked Frenchie.

"Don't think so, why?"

"Because I think we're the only fools getting wet."

That brought a smile to my face.

"Perhaps, we should pull out our ponchos?" I suggested.

"Too late for that Jersey, I'm soaked to the bone."

A jeep behind us race up to us with purpose. Someone on the front passenger side stuck his head out, "Edwards and Le Baron."

We raised our hands like we were in grade school.

Frenchie leaned towards me, "Why did we do that?"

I shrugged my shoulders. "Dumb, wasn't it?"

"Yeh, yeh. Coon ass dumb."

As I picked up my duffle bag, "I have no idea what you just said but it sounded darn cool to me."

"Laissez les bones temps ruler." said Frenchie, "Let the good times roll. Let's go."

As we speed away in the jeep the sun began to come out. The guy in the front seat introduced himself to both of us as Spec 4 Roberts and the driver as PFC Andrews. We shook hands.

So, what's your MOS, Spec 4 Le Baron?" Roberts asked.

"Sixty Seven November Twenty." said Frenchie, proudly.

"And you?"

"67Y20 Cobra Mechanic."

The jeep driver turned on his directional signal and pulled over to stop. The two of them studied me for a moment.

"You are not that 67Y20 we heard about that had an 87% score, blew the final, and didn't get promoted?"

"Yeah," said, the PFC, "he is. I remember the name with the story."

"Is that a good thing or a bad thing?"

"For us, it was awesome. For the NCOs, not. You're kind of a rebel hero."

"And, you're probably wondering why I did what I did but the word classified only makes me more mysterious?"

All three were shaking their heads up and down

Once in Nam, Always in Nam

wanting to know why I did what I did.

"Hate to disappoint but it is classified."

Fact is, had I told them the truth, it wouldn't have changed a darn thing. Had I told them that a kid I grew up with wanted me to cheat for him on the final.

When I refused to do so, he broke his red lead pencil loud enough to make it known he broke it, got me to give him mine and then waited till the last minute to give me the pencil back with the broken lead. I wound up doing two conditional Red X's, two Red X's and one red dash with a black lead.

A 100% went to a 60%. So, when they asked me what happened, I asked for my response to be off the record. They agreed, let me take the test over to prove I was telling the truth and it came out to 100%.

I basically, took a physiological bullet for my friend. He went to Germany as an E-4. At least, that's what

Before going through the back side of Camp Eagle, you couldn't help but notice the mama-sons with heir straw hats, the black dresses and their black tea stained teeth smiling at you trying to sell their weed to the GIs.

The narrowing between the hills funneled the traffic into a two-way split so that the driver would always be to the closest to the MP on either side.

Put in the same hooch with Frenchie. We dried off and changed clothes.

"You going to tell me or not?"

"You got the cheat sheet with the correct answers?"

"How did you know?"

"Intuition. But it doesn't matter."

We both made sure no one else was in the hooch.

"Okay, I have my back to you. The first is a Red X, the 4th is a circle red X as is the tenth. 16 is a red X and 20 is a red diagonal.

"Geez Louise. You didn't miss a one."

I smiled. "Now, you know. And now, I know why I'm seeing Master Sergeant Solomon at 4pm instead of right after morning chow. They already have a hard on for me and unless there is a Cobra down in the hanger, this PFC is about to be on every dirty job they can put me on."

"And just how, exactly does that wash out?"

"Told you. I'm an Army brat." I said as I walked out the hooch and headed for King Solomon's mines.

Master Sergeant Solomon was a tall lanky, technically seasoned lifer. Pleasant when he wanted to be, ball buster when he had to be. He stood up, smiled, shook my hand and told me to sit down.

"PFC Jacobs."

"Yes, Sergeant Solomon."

"Find SP6 Johnson and tell him his new 67Y20 has arrived."

I stood up, shook hands and then we both sat down.

"I don't have any Cobras for you to work on so I'm going to attach you to the slicks.

"Also, while I can't tell you to shave off your mustache I would strongly suggest that you do. My reasoning is, why cultivate hairs on your face that grow naturally on your ass."

Blinky, blink, blink, BOOM!

Not the sound you want to hear on day one at Camp Eagle.

But thank you Charlie Cong for saving me from laughing like a lunatic in the face of the this politically correct kiss up. I hate these jerks!

They are the kind of human slime that needed to be shaken and stirred. Promoted to their highest level of incompetency and never understanding why no one wants to work for them.

Because you're an idiot!

But his facial expressions of going from snot head to scared out of your wits head was TOTALLY PRICELESS!!

Not yet educated on where to go or what to do, I followed them out the door, across the road and into the bunker where they hid until the all clear was sounded. It was time to go to the mess hall. But the politically correct E-6 said something to me that made it perfectly clear where he stood.

"In all honesty, PFC Edwards, I don't want you working for me."

Imagine my surprise.

Richard T. Edwards

THE NIGHT I SALUTED SANTA

WHEN YOU GO OUT on guard duty, you go to your post, make sure your claymore mines are pointing outwards, there was at least one firing cap in it and the wires to the bunker were insulated and not exposed. You carried with you an M-16, M-79 or M209.

To put it another way, you carried a rifle, a grenade launcher or a combination of the two. You also carried your own metal boxes of ammunition with you. But the M-60 machine gun was always there and always coming with ample amounts of ammunition.

Claymore mines were interesting in that there was a thin even layer of C-4 in front of a thin wire plate. Holes in the plate held Beebe sized metal balls. When the mine exploded, it would fire these steel bee bees, out to about 100 meters within a 60° arc. The correct side facing the enemy said, "This side faces the enemy."

You would not believe how many of them faced the other direction because soldiers just didn't read the instructions.

Inside the bunker, you made sure you had a "clicker" that worked, had enough hand flares to keep you happy and the batteries in the starlight scope were new and full of power.

There could be more than one assigned to each bunker but most of the time, you were the only one there.

If you lucked out, you wouldn't be the first in the line of bunkers and you wouldn't be the last. There was also a landline that connected the bunkers to each other and all of them could be called at once by the

Richard T. Edwards

Officer of The Day.

Again, much of this equipment depended on who was responsible for the bunkers. Sometimes, a 55-gallon drum of foo gas – a mixture of explosives and napalm – was out in front of a Claymore mine.

About once a week, you would head out for guard duty and you would stay at your post until time for breakfast.

As it so happened, one of those nights was the night before Christmas and my name was on the duty roster.

Since I'm new to the ways of war zones, I expected the night before Christmas be no different than any other night. The standard routine would consist of at least three nightly challenges – mostly because the Officer on Duty wanted to make sure the troops weren't sleeping, on mad minute time slot and at least on refer idiot going nutz because a rabbit jumped across a ditch in front of him.

I think we killed more rabbits or other wild animals than enemy out in front of the outer parameter of Camp Eagle. The fur being the only reminder that it once lived.

Lord help you if a refer head found a snake inside the bunker. Imagine if you will 20 flares going off inside a bunker, followed by a screaming and hollering refer head only over shadowed by gunshots, machine guns and not to be left out, a few grenades.

Never quite sure who got more bloodied, the snake or the refer head. Personally, I don't think the snake had a chance.

Sigh.

Anyways, on the night before Christmas, Santa decided to pay us all a visit. Even the refer heads paid homage by night lighting up their bowls until after he passed.

Almost all of us knew that a Colonel or higher was

going to dress up like Santa and visit us. And when the time came, we all came out to the edge of the bunker near the edge of the road and echoed the usual "Halt, who goes there."

After that, he wished us a Merry Christmas and then I saluted Santa and said, "You do the same, Sir."

It was the Commanding Officer of the 101st Airborne Division, MG John M. Wright himself.

Richard T. Edwards

GOING TO THE TRUCK WASH

THERE IS SILENCE that steals the moment and satisfies a stare into the steal blue sky of a shiny new day. Home, red dust dirt and hell prevails.

If you timed it just right and walked briskly, you wouldn't smell it.

But you had to be quick.

Otherwise, the comfort of a new day's wealth of sweet smelling but always overcooked bacon, the morning rise and shine and freshly created nutmeg scented promise of pancakes air would shift another direction reminding one of one's usage of such delightful food goes in and must come out.

The stench of burning human waste is something you learn to understand as a fact of life when you are at Camp Eagle and there's no system of fresh water or human waste products.

The clanging of metal trays, the smell of overlay cleaned metal water bays just below the polished stainless-steel food trays and the sounds of member soldiers talking about the various letter they get from girls like a status symbol almost drown out the screaming generator providing the mess hall with its voltage lifeblood.

You sign in, take the Monday horse pill, watch the head sign in master watch you take it and then put a check mark beside your name as though the fate of your existence depended upon his ability to perform such actions.

The guys PFC whose name you could never pronounce. And you wonder where in the heck did they get these people? They are here in the morning, afternoon and evening but never see them otherwise.

What are they? Ghost, CID, or the First Sergeants lineup of bitches?

"National guard, Move on!"

I stared too long at his nametag. A slight smirk crosses my lips as I slap two pieces of toast onto the five places, pull apart two squares of butter turning slightly yellower around the edges and brace for the creamy clumps of meat and sausage mixture known as SOS.

A slight tilt of head in protest delivers a bit more but its presentation reveals disdain as the tray begins to take on all the appearance of an 18-inch gun going off on my tray.

Scrambled eggs and two pieces of bacon top off my morning intentions along with a hot black cup of coffee tasting more like a watered-down bottom of the barrel version with the grounds as topping you didn't have to pay extra for.

Plopping this steamy mess down in front of the clan of the aircraft mechanics, I focus on the milk cooler and pray there's still some chocolate milk to flavor and an extra spoon to skim off the grounds.

Ever notice how the milk on the chocolate side was always completely gone no matter what time you got to the mess hall or those rubber tubes used remind you of a cow's tit? Just without the rounded nipple at the end of it.

I should recommend this king of nozzle. All you would have to do is raise point the tit part into your mouth and hold the 20-pound sledgehammer looking weight.

Of course, if your hand slips off weight, the best-case scenario is an embarrassment lump. Worst, in a body bag.

"I'm sorry to inform you, ma am, but your son was

killed trying to drink milk from a makeshift cow's tit and his hand slipped off a 20-pound counter weight.

"We have pictures of the incident and plan on selling them to the National Enquirer.

"Sorry about your loss. Have a nice day."

Got just enough chocolate milk out of the damn thing before it dried up. Wait, did I just say that?

"Okay, Frenchie, summary report."

"One says she can't wait to fondle my balls and give me a blow job.

"Second says her mother and father can wait to meet me.

"The third says she's carrying my baby.

"The fourth says, she knows lady Frankenstein – showing us the image of the gargantuan exceeded beyond belief what our imagination of what this mound of female flesh looked like. I mean f lubber rubber with no beginning and no end. A pair of eyes in the middle the only distinguishable landmark. Are there even breasts somewhere in there?

"She can't wait to grab my ears and ...

"Okay, Frenchie, we get the idea. Just don't forget to keep your insurance policy going, you're going to need it."

I honestly had no appetite after that.

"Okay, so everyone, is it me or is something going on?"

"Didn't you hear?"

"Mushroom."

"All of the entire 36 Cobras of the 4th Battalion, 77th Field Artillery are up in the air head for the Ashu Valley."

"A surprise attach when you can hear them 5 miles away coming."

"Well, you know what they say, "Mine is not to reason.

And, we all chimed in with, "Mine is but to do or die."

I looked at my watch, "We've got 10 minutes before formation."

We all got up, made our donations for the dogs and pigs, ran our trays through the pre-clean, stacked them and left.

"PFC Edwards."

"Yes, Sergeant Valentine."

"Vehicle cleanup. Report to the stream."

"Frenchie said softly, "He really hates you."

That was only half true. Yes, he's still made at me about the destruction of 250 IBM punch cards which got mangled when I tried running them through the sorter.

But only half the truth. The other half was the fact that was my specialty was 67Y20 Cobra mechanic and we had none to work on.

So, off I went and headed down to the creek where other soldiers were and in the process of cleaning up our mules, jeeps and 3/4-ton vehicles. About an hour into scrubbing and cleaning it began.

You didn't have to be a Cobra mechanic to recognize the throaty thunder heading for us churning the air with the promise that 37 Cobras were about to fly overhead.

Everyone stopped what they were doing. Somewhere running as fast as I remember when we had some incoming rounds.

"Somebody hops into that 3/4 ton and pull it up to high ground."

I volunteered. Since I didn't have a camera and put the back end towards the deafening hammering of the air by the onslaught of 37 pairs of rotor blades.

"Oh, my Gawad! Are you seeing what I'm seeing?"

"You guys act like you've never seen a Cobra before

in your life." I was trying to keep my own emotions down. I must admit I was getting goose bumps at the same time wishing I had some earplugs.

They flew literally right above us. Then started to split up. 12 heading south, another 12 heading north and the rest turning and heading for a pad obviously not far away. A single Cobra – obviously the CO of the Battalion – separating from the 12 local Cobras and landing on his own pad further to the west.

I was spell bound. Cleaning the vehicles became a mechanical process that day and it made the time fly.

That night, I wrote:

Dear Mom,
Thanks for the fudge, it was enjoyable, and I shared it with my hooch buddies.
I saw 37 Cobras today flying in formation. An awesome sight! I wish I was working on them.
Instead, I find myself cleaning vehicles again and again because there are no Cobras to work on.
Love,
Richard

I sent that letter out that night. The next morning at morning formation.
"PFC Edwards."
"Yes, Sergeant Valentine."
"Report to Sergeant Solomon. You've got a Cobra to rebuild."
Everyone was no looking at me like I was Rudolph The Red Nose Reindeer and if I had a mirror, I probably would have been looking at myself the same way.

Master Sergeant Solomon was a tall, lanky poster child for all that would describe a lifer. And he carried a bigger stick than Winston Churchill. Soft spoken, intelligent, perceptive and very technically skilled in in helicopter terminology.

And I could easily read the reluctance in his eyes. He told me to sit down. After I did, he said:

"Normally, I wouldn't let a person of your rank anywhere near this Cobra without a team and a team leader. Much less you, who has a track record of screwing everything up that you touch. At least, that's what Sergeant Valentine's assessment of you said and I take his assessments with a grain of salt.

"So, I looked at your AIT records and they are telling me a different story. How you lost additional weight, volunteered to go to Airborne school, passed the rigorous PT Test only to be turned down because you have no depth perception test and were already on orders to come here.

"And you did it with an 87-percentile going into the final exam. You almost flunked the final exam.

"Didn't you want SP4? What happened?"

"Completely off the record and between us three."

"Off the record and between us three."

"A man by the name of Bates who lived one block away from me washed out his first time around and was going to wash out again without my help. I didn't help him. So, he broke his red led pencil and silently asked to borrow mine. The only thing I had left to do on the final is add my red X's, circle red X's and Red diagonals.

"There were 5 minutes on the clock, Bates handed me the broken red lead pencil and exited the test exam. I was dumb, I was naive, and I panicked. I should have simply raised my hand, said the pencil point was broken but as quite as that room is, since Bates lead break was loud enough for everyone to hear, me having the broken lead pencil would have meant either I was cheating for Bates or Bates was cheating for me.

"So, I filled them out in black pencil knowing damn

well they should have been filled out in red. And if I ever see Bates again I hope to see him being court martialed."

There was a slight smirk on Sergeant Solomon's face.

"Now, that makes sense. There's only two men in my unit capable of working on this Cobra. SP5 Franks and you.

"SP5 Franks is on special assignment."

He pointed at that shadowy figure now walking towards me. "This is SP6 Joe Freelove. He is your technical inspector."

We shook hands. "You have a lot to learn from him and about real world of air frame repair and in short order. Follow everything by the book – and I mean by the book.

"Grab yourself TMs-55-1520-30, 35 and 40. Ask for help when you need it and don't hesitate to borrow from time to time Specialist Freelove for some OJT time.

"Get your tool box and get to work."

"Oh, one last thing. You don't report to Sergeant Valentine any more, you report to me."

SP6 Joe Freelove looked at me with one of those looks that says everything, Screw this up and I will make you so miserable, you are going to wish you went home in a body bag.

Richard T. Edwards

REBUILDING A COBRA PART 1

THE AH-1G COBRA HELICOPTER is best described and one of the hardest helicopters to work on. Only 36 inches wide, everything is in tightly packed, impossible in some places to work on without a helping hand and has more moving parts per square inch than any other design.

When one comes in with sudden stoppage and a hard landing, from the back of the wing stores to above them, everything that's mechanical is going to be replaced. That includes the tail boom – shafts, hanger bearings, 42 and 90-degree boxes, the main rotor blade assembly, blade pitch control rods – what we call lollypops, scissors and sleeve assembly, swash plate, transmission, short shaft, and engine.

Just to name a few. Those were pulled on the first week. Starting from the locking device on the Jesus nut and ending with the removal of the tail boom section. This included adding the names of the parts to the 20-page list of red Axes, location of these parts and the bagging and tagging of all the nuts and bolts removed from each.

It took me 7 straight days of solid 20 hours per day workdays. A total of 140 hours. I was looking forward on Monday to come in, get the hydraulic team to pick up the body of the Cobra so that I could cut the safety wire on the 16 bolts holding the bent skids in place.

"Sergeant Solomon wants to see you."

Why am I getting tired of hearing that?

"You wanted to see me, Sergeant Solomon?"

He leaned back in his chair and said, "Want to

know what one of my jobs is?"

There was a smirk on his face, so I thought I'd be a little jolly. "Have a clue, Sergeant Solomon, But I'm sure I'm about to be told."

"Smart ass."

We both chuckled at that.

"That other job is making sure you don't get hurt on the job and based on what I'm seeing on the floor and what Specialist Freelove is telling me.

You've earned a get the hell out of my hanger and get some sleep cards. I don't want to see you down here until Wednesday and no more 20-hour shifts either. Stick with my normal hours. You got it?"

"Yes, Sergeant Solomon."

"Good. Get out of here."

So, I headed to my hooch. But I wasn't alone. Someone I hadn't met before was about to make his presence known to me. A SP5 by the name of Raymond Fletch. He was the section leader for the slicks maintenance team.

"So, you are the famous section leader the guys have been telling me about." I said as we shook hands.

"And you are the guy those same guys wish they could put in a box and send you back to the states," he said in such a way that spoke of respect and good nature.

"Explain to me how you managed to remove a part requiring two men. One on one side of the solid metal wall between the tail boom and the other on the opposite side cranking off the 4 nuts holding it in place."

I shrugged my shoulders.

"I safety wired a pair of vice grips to the bulkhead and used my ratchet on the other side."

"Don't let Freelove see you doing that, he'll write you up."

"But it worked."

"Just don't let Freelove see you doing that, or for that matter, anyone else see you using vice grips."

"Did you notice anything wrong with the rotor blades?"

"You were watching me eyeball them, too?"

There was a pause.

"Yeah, I did. Between 5 and 7 degrees off based on eyeballing it. Which could have been the reason for the sudden stoppage and hard landing."

"Did you tell Sergeant Solomon?"

"No."

"You need to. It's the only way that fact can be recorded as official."

"Okay, I'm going to go up to Sergeant Solomon and tell him that I just happened to notice a 5 to 7-degree forward misalignment in the rotor blades."

"You don't, I will."

"Okay, got it. By the way, where are you from?

"Philly."

"Are you serious?"

"Yes, I joined the Army in 1968 and yes, I know about you and your flying club. Trudy Haynes interviewed you and your flying club."

"Wow, small world."

And this story is about to get even stranger. He pulls out a little round can and said, "What are these?"

"A can of push pull bearings."

"For what helicopter?"

"Why are you carrying a pair of Cobra push pull bearings?"

"Because sooner or later, someone is going to need them."

And he was right. Obviously, that someone would be me. After all, why would he show me them since I was the only one assigned to his unit that was a 67Y20

Richard T. Edwards

Cobra mechanic?
    So, we talked shop and he gave me some great tips. The best one, in his pocket.
    After that, I went to sleep and slept like a baby for an entire day.

REBUILDING A COBRA PART 2

SOME THINGS HAVE GOT TO PASS. Like gas. Sometimes, when you think one's coming and you don't just get it over with all at once, it comes out sounding like a foghorn and clears out the hanger.

Luckily for me, I just did mine outside of earshot while smoking my pipe. Wild Cherry smoke perfumes over it well.

But I wasn't outside the hooch that night just because the guys didn't want to smell my exhaust system but because the men were having a full-fledged Dear John pity party complete with a stand around the center of the room confined fire as the popped tops on their favorite cold brew and burnt their cum coated letters and pictures of the girls who played them for fools.

After all, Christmas was fading towards the New Years and whatever these men sent to the gals for Christmas was becoming obvious that the letters were part of a national scam to get GIs to shell out money for their poor little family who desperately needs their little boy with an assortment of ailments not humanly possible.

Then it happened. At first, I thought I was hearing things. A single M16s firing on semi-automatic was firing at something outside of our perimeter. Next came the flairs and more M16s started making noise. Off in the distance you could hear the whine of the Cobra turbines and the blades picking up speed.

While the sirens share a reality, I was already aware of, a sobering silence replaced the pity party and the sounds of putting on flak jackets, combat helmets and slamming clips of 16 rounds into their M16.

Then some serious 40mm tracer rounds were being fired back into Camp Eagle and they were red, white and blue. The Cobras started shutting down and the night got quiet again. The All Clear sirens sounded, and the men went back to burning their bitches.

I didn't even bother with breakfast. Dogs with hangovers weren't worth messing with. They sure as shoot you and ask questions later. I grabbed a bartered for smokes John Wayne bar and headed for a hanger.

I was beginning to understand why what I was doing down at the hanger was far more important than playing social games with men from the south and more importantly, a Georgia Red Neck. Not saying I'm prejudice. But they had their ways of letting you know they were.

Why am I in Vietnam with the hostiles all around us and we, as Americans could stand each other?

When they signed you up, they never said it was going to be easy. I got that. But when the hostiles were Americans, it made you wonder what war was really being fought here the Vietnam or the Civil War?

I jumped the mud filled drainage ditch and head for my salvation: An AH-1G Cobra now torn down to just the body. No tail boom, no engine, no transmission. It was time to put her back together again from the ground up.

By the time Sergeant Solomon came to me, the new skids were under the Cobra a bolted on. Before I could start that, Sergeant Solomon has something to say.

"You need to go over to S1. A Captain Franklin needs to talk to you ASAP."

Well, that sounded serious, so I stopped everything, cleaned up my hands and headed over to S1 and had no idea what or why he'd want to talk to me.

Once in Nam, Always in Nam

Walking up the stairs, opening the door to the office I was greeted by a familiar face. So, this is where that PFC at the mess hall works.

"Ah, PFC Edwards, one moment and I'll tell Captain Franklin that you're here."

He got up, knocked on the officer's office door and was told to send me in.

I walked into his office, proceeded to salute him and stood at attention.

"At ease, PFC Edwards. Do you know what a Congressional is?"

"No sir I don't."

"Well, it boils down to the fact that any civilian – in this case, your father – can contact a public official from his state and voice a complaint that, in your particular case, you were being treated unfairly."

"Sir, I'm at a loss for words."

"Apparently your father wasn't. Says here that he, as an x US Army Recruiter himself, he knows the Army spent a good chunk of money training you on being a helicopter repairman, becoming a Cobra mechanic and wanted to know why you weren't working in your field of expertise. Citing washing vehicles, burning human waste and other unrelated activities as being demoralizing for a relative of John Clark."

"Sir, excuse my ignorance, but who the heck is John Clark?"

"Didn't they teach you about the Louis and Clark Expedition?"

"I pretty much slept through High School with two jobs and a flying club to run, sir."

"Explains why your GT score is only 105.

"There was also something else. He said he was there when the recruiter said you were signing up for 3 years, is that true?"

"Yes Sir."

"And you thought you were signing up for fixed wing training."

"Yes Sir."

"Do you really want to be in the Army, PFC Edwards?"

You know, if this question was asked of me three weeks prior before I had seen those 37 Cobras flying over, I would have said no. But with all that has happened since then and where I was at with the rebuilding of a Cobra, you'd have to hand cuff me to the bird heading stateside.

"Yes, sir."

"Then as I see it, you have 30 days to find a Cobra unit that will accept you as a Cobra mechanic or you're heading home. Dismissed."

I did a salute and walked out.

Notes to self.

Just because your mother hates your father doesn't mean the two of them aren't talking.

Don't give mom any more ammo, she already packs enough heat of her own.

What goes around, comes around.

Time to get the cobra done.

"Sergeant Solomon wants to see you in his office."

"Didn't know we had a celebrity among us."

"You don't and why do I get this sneaky suspicion that you know my father."

"We were the ones responsible in Korea for flying all the USO shows around Korea. I meant him when he was working with them and taking pictures of Debbie Reynolds in pig tails."

"I am nothing like my father."

"No," he agreed, "You are not."

"Then let me get this Cobra done."

"Who said I wasn't? What I am going to tell you is I know for a fact that B Battery, 4th Battalion, 77th

Once in Nam, Always in Nam

Field Artillery is losing 80% of is enlisted and that's where you should be able to transfer over to it. When you're waiting for the tail boom hangers to come in, go over there and tell them that Sergeant Solomon thinks you would be a good fit.

"In the meantime, rebuilt the Cobra."

I smiled at that and walked out of his office.

Richard T. Edwards

REBUILDING A COBRA PART 3

I TORE THIS BIRD from the top down. It's time to rebuild it for the bottom up.

Where's those safety wire pliers?

I'm not sure what was more fun. Taking it apart or putting it back together.

I do know one thing, the more challenging phase of this was, indeed, putting it back together.

Since Sergeant Solomon gave me two days off, I put the second in over at B Battery, 4th Battalion, 77th Field Artillery.

Seemed like everything over there spoke to me as being home.

It felt like the place had a mission to do and a keen sense of purpose. Where pure testosterone was standard operating procedure. Where a ball-busting mix of Warrant and Artillery Officers pushed their Cobras to the limits and back. And where the maintenance hangar was a buzz with all kinds of maintenance personnel putting back together what they broke.

There was a tall lanky Lieutenant in maintenance operations whom which I saluted and asked who I would have to talk to, so I could transfer over to this unit.

He pointed to a Captain and said that would be Captain Kramp. I went up to him, saluted him and told him I wanted to transfer over to his unit. He looked at me with one of his usual are your crazy looks and said, "So who sent you over here?"

I told him Master Sergeant Solomon over at A

Company, 5th Transportation. "He told me to tell you to call him if you have any questions."

"He did, did he?"

"Yes sir."

"What's your MOS?"

"67Y20, Sir"

Have you ever had one of those moments when you said something and everyone around you got deathly quiet? This was one of those moments.

"You are not the one rebuilding that Cobra all alone, are you?"

"I have had help, Sir. But yes."

"Welcome to the El Toros," he said.

I saluted, turned and walked away. I felt like a hundred eyes were watching me. What the hell was going on?

The next morning, I cornered Sergeant Solomon.

"You need to see this, please," I said with a sense of urgency. "Do you see anything wrong with these blades?"

He studied them for a moment. "No."

"If I were to take a string and go from blade tip to blade tip, you would probably see it. They aren't in line. In fact, using an eyeball estimate, there's somewhere between 4 and 6 degrees forward. And this is what most like cause the accident."

"You can see this?"

"I took 5-years' worth of mechanical drawing in High School, I'm a stickler for accuracy."

"Okay, take it down to prop and rotter and let them balance it. We must put it back on anyway. Let them tell us just how far out of alignment it was."

Came back as being 4.5 degrees off alignment. One of those shinier moments.

A week later, I was told my move was approved and a week after that, I was packing my duffle bag with my belongings. The same day the Huey team took to the task of checking all of what I did on the Cobra now standing proud and complete.

"PFC Edwards, Sergeant Solomon wants to see you before you go."

"I'm on my way."

I put my duffle bag down and walked across the street to the hanger where Sergeant Solomon was waiting for me.

"I want you to look. A real hard, long look."

There was a Huey mechanic about to put the flag up so the rotor blades would hit the mooring tips against the duct tape with red and blue markings. That's how we balanced rotor blades.

"The normal estimated time to go from where that Cobra entered our hanger to this moment in time is 320-man hours."

"So, I was right on time?"

"For 6 men doing the main frame work."

"Oh."

"PFC Edwards, I don't want you going anywhere."

"You are serious, aren't you?"

"As a heart attack. You know when you first arrived, I labeled you as a dud. I was seriously wrong. And I don't admit that often. I'll let you work on anything you want to work on."

"What about that congressional?"

"We can work around it, please stay."

I thought about it for a moment. "Sergeant Solomon, you gave me a chance to prove myself and I appreciate that, but my heart if telling me a change with a fresh start is something I need to do."

"Well, if you ever change your mind, you know who to come to."

I smiled, shook his hand and said, "Thank you, Sergeant Solomon for everything."

Richard T. Edwards

That would be the last time I would ever see him again.

It was the longest, loneliest 15-minute walk of my life going to the Headquarters building of the 4th Battalion, 77th Field Artillery.

But you know what the biggest complement was? I saw that AH-1G Cobra come in for refueling. I watched it fly smoothly over my head, transition and move with precision sideways and then just as clean, touch the ground smooth as glass.

It gave me goose bumps. And I almost dropped my bag in amazement.

It was then that I vowed, no matter what happens over the course of then next 6 months. No one could take away what I know I did and saw what I just saw.

It was time to write a new chapter. Welcome to the El Toro's!

REASSIGNED TO B BATTERY, 4/77ᵀᴴ FIELD ARTILLERY (ARA)

I SWEAR, If I had known Sergeant Valentine was coming to B Battery, 4th Battalion, 77th Field Artillery, I would have told Master Sergeant Solomon, yes.

Of course, the first crappy job that came up, he volunteered me for it. I was now riding shotgun on a trash truck, which could be stinky, stanky and stunky.

After you get past the stench and the humiliation. You begin to realize just how much C-4 (that's plastic explosive) was being carried by our soldiers and how much of it was getting thrown away. Way I calculated it, if the C-4 ever blew up, it would create one hell of a stink bomb.

"Ma'am, I regret to inform you that your son was killed in action protecting a trash truck. There wasn't enough of him to fill a condom."

Come to think of it, riding shotgun on a trash truck did have its fringe benefits.

French/Vietnam women are living angels with devil minds. One I rode with had a gritty high-pitched voice. Constantly telling me I was NUUM BER ONE.

With that said, after two weeks of being shot gun on a trash truck, one of my hooch buddies convinced me to talk a lieutenant by the name of Lt. Craig Gies.

Lt. Craig Gies stood straight as an arrow and was 6'2" tall.

Most of the time you expect guys his size that fit the description as being tall and athletic as also being, well, not so smart: A kind of Mice and Men stereotype.

This guy was not only a big man; he was extremely intelligent and cunning.

So, his nickname "The Animal" didn't make much sense. That is, until you really started knowing the man.

This was the kind of leader you would not question. The kind of man you want on your team. The kind of soldier you'd expect would become a hero.

His only flaws:

He was brutally right all the time.

He was aggressive as hell in doing the right thing all the time.

He was dedicated to pushing his soldiers under his command into rare areas of their potential they didn't even know they could do.

He also knew poker and knew how to play a serious bluff.

So, I talked to him and explained my situation. He listened. Then told me there was an opening for a crew chiefs job and said he would test me to see if I would be a good fit.

That took me off the trash truck duty. But I never did get the crew chief job.

The truth is, Lt. Craig Gies saw two physical flaws in me and after looking at my military test scores he decided for me that proved to be another brilliant moment for the both of us.

The primary reason why I didn't become an aviator was because of my lazy left eye. When I get tired, my eye turns in. And I was tired that day we met.

When I'm uncomfortable with a situation or not as secure with my environment, I say stupid things, do dumb things and otherwise appear to be scatter brained.

So, when he asked me where the RMI was in the Cobra. I couldn't find it.

Why?

It doesn't exist.

In Vietnam, Cobras were not certified for IFR or instrument flight rules flying. The radio magnetic indicator (RMI) would be in the cockpit if they were.

So, based on this Lt. Craig Gies offered me a job as an aircraft maintenance clerk. It was better than riding shotgun on a trash truck. So, I took it.

I worked the maintenance job during the day and the flight line at night. Between times, I learned how to play a mean game of Ping-Pong.

We lost two Cobras and two officers in March. The loss of two pilots and one Cobra happened the day I arrived. The loss of the second Cobra occurred when Richard Femrite decided to land his perfectly good helicopter inside the middle of a NVA base camp. Basically, what we fondly call an idiot light came on warning Femrite of no oil pressure.

He was asked by the Operations Officer if the oil temperature had increased and was told no.

Because it was up to the pilot and not the Operations Officer, Femrite elected to land the helicopter. He just picked the wrong spot to do it.

Fred Capo had to land beside the doomed chopper and pick Femrite and Maxsom using his rocket pod wing stores and skid. He then dropped the pilots off in a safe location, called a medevac and went back over to where the doomed Cobra was located.

A very pasty white Joe Maxsom jumped out of the medevac after it landed on our tarmac.

APRIL

I'm beginning to gain some respect. Especially, my antics on the flight line. After the two-minute section came in on a fire mission on late afternoon, I started to tie down the main rotor to the tail. I turned the blades the way I was trained to do but pulled them too far.

So, I had to pull the blades towards the opposite direction. There was something wrong with the engine and I pointed it out to Lt. Craig Gies.

The Cobra was pulled off the flight line and the damaged engine was replaced.

GETTING IN AIR TIME FOR AN AIR MEDAL

YOU HEAR A LOT OF WAR STORIES from Vets about their first experience with incoming rounds and how the dealt with the fact that they were being fired upon by a hostile enemy.

Well, for me, these wasn't my first experience with incoming rounds. Nor would it be my last.

I don't make it a habit of tempting fate. So, taking one's life into one's hand so to speak isn't something a take lightly.

However, for us Cobra crew chiefs and mechanics, the only way you were going to get an air medal was if you volunteered for flying door gunner or as a front seat warmer in an OH-6.

An OH 6 had 5 main rotor blades and proved to be one of the best crash able and walk away from helicopters in Vietnam. Indeed, the Cavalry loved using them as they could force the enemy to shoot at it.

Which, of course, was a bad mistake as flying circles above the aggravated enemy were to Cobras just waiting to roll in and telling the enemy all about the mistake they just made.

The OH-6 got its nickname – tadpole – because of its shape. But it was also light and agile and very response to a tug on the collective.

Which was pulled after smoke was dropped onto the target by the crew chief in the back seat.

So, if the North Vietnamese thought this little helicopter was annoying. I can only imagine the horror in their eyes when those two Cobra gunships provided them with a dinner of led.

So, this OH-6 lands on our bullpen, Lt. Craig Gies

Richard T. Edwards

yells at me to suit up and grab a flight helmet.

Few minutes later, I get in with my nomex gloves, uniform and a flight helmet. After securing the monkey strap safety harness around me, I plug in.

"Can you hear me?"

"Yes, sir."

"Good, don't touch a thing."

"Yes, sir."

We flew over to the 2/17 Cavalry refueling area and landed.

"Hang tight, I'll refuel."

I nodded with understanding.

Once refueled, the Captain made a call, scribbled some numbers on the Plexiglas and we were on our way to Fire Base T-Bone.

T-Bone wasn't but about 15 minutes north of our location. Indeed, almost parallel with Hue. Within minutes, we were getting permission to land. As I watched him land, I noticed just how good he was coordinating the pedal collective and cyclic controls and just how smooth this helicopter flew.

Once the skids touched the ground, the pilot put the collective down flat, I heard him say something about coming but the first part of that I didn't get. All I saw was helmet and ass and gone.

After that I also thought it odd that no one was outside manning the 105 howitzers. And the white puffs of smoke inside the area made some noise but were barely heard. Flight helmets block out a lot of noise. I could barely hear anything.

When all of that subsided, the Vietnamese men responsible for manning the 105s came out of the bunkers including the pilot.

They were all laughing at me.

The pilot got back into the helicopter and plugged in.

"Didn't you hear what I said?"
"No, Sir."
"I said, 'In coming,'"

I shrugged my shoulders. As far as I was concerned, I was enjoying the fireworks.

Looked back at the cannon cockers firing back at the enemy.

It was at this point in my time in Nam that I realized, I no longer feared Vietnam nor were my nerves fractured by what combat produces.

I'm never certain why that Captain didn't care if I lived or died.

I was also given the task of cleaning and polishing up a white phosphorous 10-pound rocket and stencil it with the number 2,000,000. It was to be fired later that month as a publicity stunt.

The one thing I learned about these rockets is that once you turn them 200 times, they are armed.

So, I went back and forth with only one turn.

This one still makes me laugh.

Sergeant Valentine. "Wow, PFC Edwards, that round looks really nice. How many times did you turn it?"

"You know, Sergeant Valentine," I said as a matter of fact. "I stopped counting after 230 times."

I looked back, and the pale faced Valentine creped slowly backwards out of the room where I was working.

I loved every minute of that one.

Richard T. Edwards

THOSE PUSH PULL BEARINGS IN MY BUDDY'S POCKET SAVE THE DAY

THERE WAS A HOT FIX that called for the removal of the split cone push pull bearings and the replacement of those with a new single piece bearing set.

The problem with this is the fact that once you pulled off the split cone bearings, you couldn't use them again. These were high tolerance bearings. So, pulling them off and using them again was not an option.

Well, as fate would have it, the solid set failed impressively. As a result, another directive was issued, and the split cone bearings were to replace them. Only one problem, there wasn't enough of them.

The interesting thing about this story was the fact that my buddy over at A Company, 5th Transportation Battalion would not have been aware of the immediate urgency what he had in his pocket was about to become. Had he, I think he would have upped the bargaining chips.

So, with not enough of them to go around, CPT Denny Kramp, Lt. Craig Gies, and SFC Valentine had a meeting of the minds about 12 feet away from me.

"I'm telling you there aren't anymore. I've checked with all the supply units up and down here and Saigon. No one has them."

"Can't we just put the old one back on?"

"It will be your neck, not mine. They fail, and we

lose our jobs."

"Excuse me, but what is it that you need."

"This is a private conversation and none of your business."

I just listened while I acted like I was doing something.

"Okay, so what do we do?"

"Well if we can't get the part, pretty much our careers are over as we won't be combat ready."

"Sergeant Valentine, are you sure no one in Vietnam has a pair of split cone bearings."

"Yes, sir. Nobody has a new set."

"I can find you a pair."

"Didn't I just tell you to shut up?"

"Do you want the part or not?"

"Oh, alright, take the jeep and don't come back if you can't find a pair."

I grew to love Lt. Craig's ultimate do or die attitude. So, I got into the jeep, rode across the flight line and drove over to a very familiar area.

I had to wait a few moments for everyone to come in from work. I smelled the pipe before I saw the man.

"Hi."

"Suppose you want what's in my pocket."

"Okay either you're psychic or simply know the only time I come over here is when I want something?

"The second would be the more appropriate answer. What will you give me for it?"

Way I see it, if I was an officer whose career and fate was about to be changed, I'd offer him a ride in the Cobra, since he just saved my ass.

But I wasn't. So, I said, "How about a case of beer?"

"You know I don't drink beer," he scolded.

"Okay, a case of Cokes."

"That will work," he said as he pulled them from out of his pocket.

Once in Nam, Always in Nam

"Mind if I bring the Cokes over tomorrow?"

"Not at all." he retorted. "Tomorrow will be fine."

He handed them to me. I then shook his hand and said, "See you tomorrow."

A few minutes later, I parked the jeep, turned it off, walked up to the three men and handed them the part. The picture in my mind of the jaws dropping pretty much said it all.

At the time, I just wanted to help and keep my Battery combat ready.

I had no idea how that moment in time was about to shape my future in more ways I could have dreamed possible.

My R&R got approved for the last week in April. So, orders came in and within a few weeks, I would be on my way to Japan and the Worlds Expo in Osaka.

Richard T. Edwards

EXPO 70

WHILE MOST SOLDIERS were heading to Australia for – essentially – sex, I was headed to Osaka, Japan to – essentially, enjoy the country and see the World's Fair there.

Next day, I was on the Bullet Train heading for Osaka, Japan. It was a three-hour train ride covering 450 miles. Back in those days, that was one hell of a fast train. Once I arrived at Osaka, I headed over to the Plaza International Hotel and booked my room for the next 5 days.

The World's Fair wasn't in or near the main parts of Osaka. Instead, it was in a town called New Sentry. To get there, you had to catch a train from the main train station and ride it for several miles before actually arriving at the World's Fair area.

There was a huge number of things to see and very visually pleasing attractions for everyone. Designs and expressions in architecture were unusual to say the least.

As you waked into Fair, the first thing you noticed was the tall Japanese sculpture standing high in front of the entrance walkway.

It looked like a modern-day handle for a hair dryer. Round and wide at the bottom, narrower and bent forward at the top. It was white with red stripes, and from this neck like top was a gold sculpture of the sun god. The theme of the fair was "Progress and Harmony for All Mankind."

I wasn't quite sure if that theme meant anything to anyone considering where I just came from.

The most interesting sites to see were:

The US Pavilion, which was designed to look, like

a Hawaii volcano. It had an air-supported roof. So, you had to go in and out of the building through locks. For the most part, the USA pavilion was a physical walk through Life Magazine.

The Canadian Pavilion which included a Canadian Mounty on his horse outside the Pavilion. Inside, there were interesting art displays, including a very large bear who would occasionally come alive and scare everyone – including me. Dioramas showed how life in Canada was at that time. There was also a movie covering the history of the country.

The Swiss Pavilion was a large glass and light structure which was pretty but made no sense.

I will never forget when a Japanese young man yelled out, "Ken tucker fir did chr ken."

The walkways were roomy the place was very open and there was plenty for me to see and do for days on end.

The most significant moment was when I became friends with an employee from the Canadian Pavilion and he invited me to stay at his apartment the next time I would come to the Fair. That coupled with the fact that I wanted to see the 5th Dimension at the concert hall at the fair was enough for me to return to the Expo in September.

I left Osaka late on April 31st. Got up to Tokyo before midnight, caught the train to my destination and the trains stopped running.

So, I called the Navy MPs, told them my situation. They picked me up and called the Army MPs. The Army MPs picked me up around 4:30 and proceeded to get lost.

In fact, after I found out that the 5th Dimension were going to be coming to the EXPO, the Canadians from the Canadian Exhibit invited me to stay at their apartment because they knew I wouldn't be able to find an empty hotel.

Where I had issues was when I went back up to Tokyo and the trains stopped running. So, I called the Navy MPs. They picked me up and then they called the Army MPs. They picked me up and proceeded to get lost.

Since the planes switched from North to South Vietnam every other day, I didn't fly back into Da Nang on the 2nd of May 1970 but rather to Saigon.

Richard T. Edwards

HEADING BACK FROM SIGON

SO, AFTER COMING BACK LATE from R&R, relieved that my polished rocket hadn't been responsible for the mayhem which was everywhere, my primary concern was to find out exactly what happen and if everyone I knew was all right – even Valentine.

Consequently, the first thing I did was secure my personal belongings. My hooch as closest to the main road leading into the Battery area. And since everyone was up or around ground zero, technically I wasn't back yet. Which also meant, officially, I was counted as missing in action.

Guess I better explain that one. Okay, yours truly had built a reputation of being either up on the flight line or silently working on making sure everything and everyone was happy. So, the powers that were assumed I was either there that morning when the attack occurred – 2:30 am and got vaporized or I was just nowhere to be found. Which also meant I was a KIA or killed in action.

I can assure you that a ghost is not writing this.

Luckily, no one got killed that morning. That was a big relief. But we were missing a hanger, about 5 Cobras, a TOC, and around 500 2.75 rockets.

Okay we weren't missing them. They were everywhere they weren't supposed to be.

Indeed, almost every hooch was decorated with a rocket or two. Some managed to penetrate through the metal and sandbags others just logged themselves into the sides.

It was as though someone from hell decided to

decorate the unit with a new kind of porcupine art only the devil himself would appreciate.

There was some noise coming from the hooch across from mine. Heavy footsteps, barely audible cursing. I recognized the voice. It was Pennsylvania. He and I had become friends and he had just gotten back from his 30 leave. He was a tall man and built. The kind of guy you would want on your side if there was any real fighting to be done. He was our truck mechanic.

"Hey Jersey. See what I've got to come back to." He pointed to the hole in the wall just above where his body would be lying down on his sleeping cot. "Damn thing missed me by inches. Hit the floor and started spinning around."

There were burnt marks on the floor.

"Geese, what did you do?"

"Kicked it out of the door."

I'm thinking the reply to that one, "I regret to inform you that your son was killed when a 2.75-inch rocket entered his hooch and blew it up to smithereens. You son included. Oh, forgot to mention the they were the US Army rockets?"

"Anyone get killed?"

"Nope. Hell, of a night, hell of a day. Geis was looking for you. They thought you were dead. Says he's got a job for you. One you might like…if you were still breathing."

"Well, I guess I am. Thanks."

"Yeah, yeah. Go find Geis."

Walking up to ground zero was like walking onto a movie set. It just didn't seem real. The two-minute section Cobras were where they were supposed to be, they just didn't look like Cobras any more. In front of them was the smoldering ruins of our hanger. The TOC was a porcupine.

I was staring at the mess when a voice behind me

brought me to attention. It was our commanding Officer.

"Specialist Edwards."

"Yes, sir"

"You are alive."

No sir I'm a born-again holograph.

"Yes sir."

"Great! Lt. Geis has a job for you, Report to him ASAP."

"Yes, sir"

I my mind at that moment I wasn't thinking in terms of anything but, what is it this time another shot gun job. Anyway, it's not hard to spot Geis out of a crowd. And a lot of them were snapping pics of the wrecked Cobras.

"Lt. Geis, Sir."

He pulls me over to the side and says, "Dick, I have a job for you."

Okay, only time someone calls me that is when we've created a serious commitment to getting something done. Something that isn't in the rulebooks. Something that must get done. Something that crosses the boundaries of rank and Army rules and regulations.

"See that jeep over there," he points, "It's yours. I'm fitting it with a radio." He pulls his CEOI book off from around his neck and hands it to me. "Carry this. Put it around your neck"

"Your job from now until completion is to help me rebuild this unit. You are to beg; borrow or steal anything you can get your hands on that will get us back up and running. If you get caught stealing, I'll bail you out of jail. Go, do your thing."

It's amazing how finding one pair of split cone bearings and persistence impacted not only this moment in time but the rest of my life.

May 4th and 5th

My new job found me running back and forth from my new home to my old one about a time in one day. Going empty and coming back with tech manuals, helicopter parts and logbooks.

So, there wasn't too much time to get sleep and only time to adhere to SFC Valentine's mid-day roll call. But I was there when he told us that the unit officially was in stand down mode. And after formation, I convinced CPT Douglas N. Winfrey that I would pay him back for a cold Coco-cola.

Winfrey was one of a few officers who would talk to an enlisted man as a human being. And as we got closer, he showed me pictures of his nine-month-old girl and wife.

Anyway, later in the evening of May 4th, I grabbed a cup of coffee from the pot in the logistics section over at A Company, 5th Trans and conducted my usual social conversations to warm them up into saying yes to my request for parts and supplies.

I never got to that point in the conversation because two seemingly insane words came over the radio: "Fire Mission".

The longer version of this is essentially was. "You have a fire mission. The grid coordinates are the following...."

By the time he got to that, I was in my jeep and on my way back over to the flight line. In less than two minutes I was on the flight line and watched Jeffery Johns leave the pad without a front seat. Winfrey was yelling at me to get his front seat.

The was the Warrant Officer 1 – we call a "wobbly one" which was having a hard time of it getting his flak jacket and such by the name of WO1 Dean L. Bonneau. I picked him up and brought him over to the Cobra. I then closed the gunner canopy. While closing the pilots, I said, "When you get back, I'll buy you a coke.

Once in Nam, Always in Nam

Winfrey smiled as I secured the latch.

I had no idea that I would be the last to see him smile. As I watched the helicopter fly away I thought it odd that the anti-collision lights were not on but then realized we might not want to raise that kind of attention from the enemy.

I went back over at A Company, 5th Trans and started chit chatting with the guys behind the counter.

"I thought you guys were stood down?"

"Yeah, so did I. Apparently DIVARTY didn't get that message."

My problem with my radio is I can hear more from the air than I can from the ground over distance. I would not have heard the Division Artillery call had that signal been a normal radio transmitter.

I'm also capable of hearing two conversations at once and reacting to both. After going to the R&R Center and talking with Johns, hearing his voice on the radio...there was something terribly wrong.

From http://www.armyaircrews.com/cobra_nam.html
CPT Douglas N. Winfrey
WO1 Dean L. Bonneau
Thua Thien Province
B/4/77 ARA
#67-15620

Mid-air with flare ship UH-1 68-16244. Nave lights were not operational.

"I've got to go."

I was weird not having a hanger to guide my way at night over on the flight line. Just as equally eerie the deathly quiet. But I found my way over to the mini officer's club turned into our Battery's tactical operations center (TOC).

Since it was our TOC and since I usually don't

knock on TOC doors, I swung open the door and was about to say something stupid like what the hell is going on. Instead, I saw something I was not supposed to see. Our CO and a huddled bunch of officers were huddled around the radio. Some in shock, others with tears rolling down their faces.

Of course, the CO saw me starring and yelled for someone to get me out of there. I just let myself out.

"Dick."

"Yes, sir."

"You know what just happened."

"Somewhat."

"You okay?"

"No. But I'm pissed so, that will work in my favor now, sir."

"Good, you're 13 Echo. Use your lights to bring in Jeffery. Have him land and put the Cobra park the Cobra. I'm giving you a command order to pull him out of the helicopter if you must. Take him over to the field Dispensary and bring him back. Go to bed. I will tell Valentine to leave you alone. Get some sleep."

"Yes sir."

So, I sat in my jeep in the middle of our pad waiting for a call and feeling kind of weird about having to deal with Jeffery. But I did. And sure enough, I had to tell him to get out of the Cobra.

Now, you got to figure a guy with a 45 who just witnessed two of his friends get killed in a mid-air over Firebase Nancy is not going to be someone you want to pull rank on. But I managed to pull it off. Got yelled at all the way to the dispensary and back about how E-4s don't talk to officers that way.... blah, blah, blah.

Finished up tying down the Cobra and went to bed. I think I was barley asleep when some jerky PFC kicked my cot. You don't kick my cot. You never kick my cot. I looked up at the PFC.

"Sergeant Valentine wants...
I didn't let that ##$#@$ PFC even finish.
"You tell Valentine to go get $@@$."
"I will..." and he went running out the door. Okay, I got back into present time and realized I was still in the Army and telling your favorite SFC to get #$#$# wasn't exactly a good career move.

I could hear Valentine, "He said WHAT?"

I was then ordered into the orderly room where Valentine proceeded to do the "I'm not putting up with this #$#$." Upon completion of his rat, the First Sergeant told him to get out of his orderly room.

"Future Specialist Edwards. I know what you did last night. They're putting you in for some awards.

So, I'm only going to tell you this once. You ever tell one of my senior NCOs to get #$#$#, I will throw the book at you. Is that clear?"

"Yes, First Sergeant."

"Good, now, get out of my orderly room and do what Lt Geis has order you to do."

Implying get some sleep.

I came to attention, saluted and walked out. Went back to bed. From that point on Valentine was no longer my boss. Lt. Craig Gies was.

BTW, 7 people were killed that night on a practice Red Alert over Firebase Nancy. The two Cobra pilots and the five people on board the UH-IH flare ship.

Jeffery Johns did apologize for acting like a horse's ass that night and my last encounter with him was indeed chummy. He apparently decided that a Cobra that wasn't signed off yet as being worthy had to go on a mission and – despite protest by the mechanics – flew off with it.

Five minutes later, he brought it back with one of the rocket pods hanging down.

He got out and proceeded to chew out the

mechanics. I just couldn't stop laughing ... same old Jeffery Johns. As he walks by me: "They're trying to kill me. I've got 2 weeks left in country and they're trying to kill me."

Snicker, snicker, and in a low voice he could only here. "You did it to yourself, Jeffery Johns."

"Yeah, I know ..." he said tapping on my shoulder.

We never saw each other again.

COMMAND AND CONTROL NORTH

WHILE I WASN'T EXACTLY INVOLVED with these missions, I was involved with the mechanical support of the AH-1G Cobras that were involved in them.

Command and Control of the North (CCN) missions where flown out of Quang Tri, approximately 56 miles north of Hue. Highway 1 would get you there if you were driving.

Below is the military description of CCN:

Reconnaissance missions were flown out of Quang Tri to penetrate positions in North Vietnam, Laos and Cambodia. Our mission was to fly with the UH-1H Hueys who would drop off a mixture of special forces NCOs and combinations of American, Korean "Rock" soldiers, and Vietnamese soldiers (a total of 9); all of whom wore and carried unmarked clothing and equipment, to maintain plausible deniability.

Our Cobras where used to support the Hueys while they dropped off and picked up the men. These men were dropped off and picked up using ropes, monkey ladders and landing zones. All were considered hot.

From my perspective, this was a real as it gets. My one and only experience with this mission was to fabricate a hydraulic line from scratch, be flown up to Quang Tri, remove the line that took a bullet and replace it with the one I created.

I had no idea what a CCN or what our Cobra mission was. I just knew I had to fix the line to get the Cobra back up in the air.

The rest of the month was pretty much a routine of going back and forth to A Company, 5th Trans, moving our Cobras over to that location and making sure both me and Lt. Craig didn't get thrown into jail for some of the crazy antics we pull off.

I'm not quite certain on some of the dates but between May and the middle of July, I basically rebuilt the Battery from the Administration side and the Sea Bees built it back from the physical side.

Also, during that same period, I moved the two-minute section over to A Troop, 2/17th Cav and fabricated a 3/8-inch hydraulic line, flew up to the CCN pad in Quang Tri and replaced the line that took a round in it with the fabricated one.

FIREBASE RIPCORD

FIREBASE RIPCORD was the last full confrontation between the US and the North Vietnamese.

It involved the 101st Airborne talking over an abandoned Marine firebase. The bold paragraphs are from the official after-action report.

Fire Support/Operational Base RIPCORD was to be opened on or about 1 April 1970 as a key forward fire support/operational base in the division's summer offensive plans against the 803d and 29th NVA Regiments in the A SHAU VALLEY area. Mutually supporting firebases would be opened at FSB BRADLEY (105mm how) and AIRBORNE (105mm how). AIRBORNE, in turn, was within mutually supporting range of FSB KATHRYN (155mm how).

Any notion that the firebase could provide the type of support the planners intended roll ended abruptly when on July 18 a CH-47 Chinook helicopter was shot down on the firebase.

The helicopter crashed in a 105mm ammunition storage area and burst into flames. The resulting fire and exploding artillery ammunition destroyed 5 105mm howitzers, 2 106mm recoilless rifles, one mechanical mule, and several other items of equipment. The remaining 105mm howitzer on the firebase was damaged.

This is where the 4th Battalion, 77th Artillery enters the picture. While C Battery up at Camp Evans was more involved with this mission, Cobras from both B Battery and A Battery were also engaged in a non-stop 24x7 ARA assault on enemy targets.

Heavy 12.7mm anti-aircraft fire was directed against the aircraft flying into the firebase. Air, artillery, and ARA destroyed several enemy mortars and 12.7mm machineguns. In addition, numerous enemy driven into the open by CS were killed by air, artillery, and ARA.

The picture above shows me and another soldier loading rockets into an A Battery Cobra as our Battery Commander looked on. To say we were busy was an understatement.

ENEMY LOSSES. From 13 March through 23 July, the enemy suffered 422 NVA KIA, 6 NVA PW, and 93 individual and 24 crew-served weapons captured.

FRIENDLY LOSSES. During the same period, US losses were 68 KIA and 443 WIA.

Casualties during the extraction on 23 July were 3 KIA and 20 WIA.

I was glad that B Battery didn't lose a single Cobra during that period. For once in my life I felt like I was a part of something bigger than life. That we were able to not only rebuild our unit but could respond to this kind of mission after almost losing everything in the rocket attack we had on May 3rd is just an amazing story.

Looking back at it now, while there are no awards or decorations for doing the job I did, knowing I was where I was supposed to be is the biggest reward I can take with me to my grave.

SO WHY ARE YOU WHISPERING?

BELIEVE ME, I couldn't make this one up if I tried. Although a couple of journalists have tried to place this incident later, the fact is, this incident happened while I was still with B Battery, 4th Battalion, 77th Field Artillery.

I also wrote it up as one of my very first stories I did as a stringer for the Battalion. And, it is totally true.

Apparently some ARVNS – those are the Vietnamese friendlies – observed some – 208 – NVA – enemy soldiers – take shelter in some empty huts. Hearing one of our Cobras they talked to the pilots that I could hear with my radio. Unfortunately, I couldn't hear the ground chatter.

The key response that got me back in the jeep and head for all sorts of euphoric chaos was a question the pilot asked: "Why are you whispering?"

When that pilot started whispering back I was gone.

I think everything that was flyable was up in the air that day and us guys on the ground were running back and forth across the flight line to keep the Cobras armed with plenty of rockets. Some of the Cobras weren't from B Battery, too.

With the ARVNS on the ground, we were able to get an accurate kill count. The tally was 208 with no friendlies killed.

A hell of a day.

When the new Transportation Commander took over and asked if my job was really needed anymore, Lt. Craig Gies looked at me and I knew from that look that a new job was percolating in his head.

As it turned out, I became the public affairs stringer for the 4th Battalion, 77th Field Artillery. A job that would eventually have me record the Cobra's development and deployment as a TOW Missile firing platform in Europe.

By the time I left B Battery and went to Battalion for my new job as a stringer, Firebase Ripcord had just happened, and the focus was on awards and decorations. So, the first day was an interesting one to say the least.

We flew up to Camp Evans where I took an image of an OH-58 being flown back from Ripcord under the belly of a CH-47. I also took some images of the officers being given awards during the awards and decorations ceremony.

When I returned I found out that SFC Ford would be my new boss.

Of course, SFC Ford, like Valentine, thought he owed me.

I don't know why I was assigned to S-3. All I know is it wasn't me how showed him the errors of his ways. It was Command Sergeant Major Jones.

One thing you learn quick is you don't mess with a Command Sergeant Major. Especially one by the name of Jones. CSM Jones was a burly black man who loved to find stuff that wasn't secure and would take it and make it his.

When this happened, you learned quickly to secure your equipment and more importantly, when it is your camera.

When Jones found out that Ford had me doing things I wasn't there to do, Jones made sure that would not happen again.

There was also an awkward time when I was between orders. I wasn't exactly the Battalion Stringer just yet. And a lot of things can happen in just a few short weeks,

HEADED TO EAGLE BEACH

"OH, THAT EXPLAINS EVERYTHING. Damn sure not in the US, are we?"

"Name's Bordeaux. Yours?" he asks as he spits out his chewing tobacco.

"Edwards."

"Yankee from the sound of it. Might want to remove your watch. Easy steal. Better in your pocket than nowhere."

I started pulling off the watch, "So where are you from?"

"Louisiana. Cajun coon ass through and through."

His words were flavored with French and brewed from the bayou.

He went through the low medium and high gears with so much precision you could barely feel the cab twist and raise by the torque.

"Guess you're going over to Eagle Beach by the looks of your clothes. And you aren't infantry, you smell too goofy to be a grunt."

I smiled. "I'm with the 4th Battalion, 77th Field Artillery. Cobra mechanic but I'm working as a stringer for the battalion."

"What in tarn nation is a stringer?"

"I'm a writer and photographer for the unit."

"Oh," he said sounding a bit disappointed. "Wanna coke?"

He pointed behind the seat, "Cooler back there. Grab one for me whale you're at it."

I did, and we popped the tops of some ice-cold body satisfaction. It was hot, muggy and the fine dust made your sweaty skin feel like sandpaper.

"I'll take you up to where the vehicles cross by LST. You'll have to jump into a duce and a half to get across," he said.

"Appreciate that."

There was a few minutes' worth of silence as we literally, drank down the cola without breathing once.

"So, tell me something, Bordeaux, how long have you been driving on highway one?"

"For almost nine months. And let me tell you something. This place has to get better to die," he was deadly serious.

"Son, let me tell you what, if you're a Vietnamese, you better not be riding a moped and get involved in an accident. Even if you don't get hurt bad. You will be by the time it's all over.

"And if you're unconscious, you'll wake up naked or dead. Or both.

"They'll plum rob you dead." He shook his head, "I've never seen anything like it. Some of those Vietnamese are like human vultures just waiting for road kill."

After we got out of Hue, he put his boom box between us and it started playing the Cajun version of American Bandstand. I started singing, if only to myself, I can't wait till I get out of his truck cause Cajun ain't that cool.

I still think I could hear his music a quarter of a mile away from sight over the hammer of his diesel.

The air smelled of fish oil and LST exhaust. You could see and hear the fish jumping out of the water. A few minutes later, I was in the back of a duce and a half and riding the LST across to Eagle Beach.

Since I had already been to Eagle Beach before, I discovered that while I was supposed to be there all day relaxing and having a good time, I couldn't wait to get

Once in Nam, Always in Nam

away and ride the roads of adventure.

Unfortunately, someone I knew saw me and I had to ride back in one of the trucks that brought the infantry up to Eagle Beach. As luck would have it, most found a way to pour themselves into the back of the first truck leaving those who didn't drink. Way I saw it, the exhaust breath of the drunks could have fueled the duce and a half all the way back to Camp Eagle.

Richard T. Edwards

THE NIGHT I WATCHED 5 SOLDIERS DIE

IT MAY HAVE HAPPENED LATE one evening or early the next day, in July 1970. All I know is it happened, and I watched every minute of it in horror. It was like watching a Vietnam movie only every second was real.

We have a lot of units around our area. From my hooch next to the road, I can see the 159th Chinook pad, the slicks from the 101st Aviation battalion and watch them all come into the refueling point.

Usually, when the air is calm of all the helicopter blades popping and chopping up the air, I listen to the ADA 175mm guns firing out going rounds in stereo and try to tune out the steady generators screaming hot exhaust into the air.

Sometimes, too, when local life hasn't been bombarded with all the man-made noises, I listen to the crickets and frogs in the swamp and smack the crap out of the Kama Cazzie vampire who attack as fiercely as we do with our Cobras.

That night was one of those hot, muggy summer nights where you couldn't fall asleep until you were too tired to care if the devil himself was in your hooch cooking your pitch forked body in hell like a marshmallow.

A clear night, you could see the stars.

It wasn't the first clunk of the B-40 motor firing that got my attention. It was the third that told me these rounds weren't ours and they were being fired very close to our outside parameter where our guards were. I counted a total of 15.

Our troops hit those bastards so fast, hard and

furiously with everything they had that for one split second, my focus was not on the 2/320th stand down area.

But when the first round hit inside the CQ's building of the 2/320th, I realized the rounds weren't coming our way. And as the rounds continued to hit the area, the red fire of the round, silhouetted men trying to run into bunkers.

I watched and listened to the hot metal fragments fly and penetrate metal and flesh. Screams seared through the thunder. The air grew cold, heavy. Death was on the doorstep as the reaper harvested their souls.

The sirens of an attack finally filled the air of Camp Eagle and I went back to work diving. Lt. Craig Gies around our interior guard positions.

"Okay, Dick, you don't look your usual self. What's going on?"

"What's going on," I said, not giving a damn about rank, "is I just watched a mortar attack hit the 2/320th across the street.

"In-other-words, Lt. Gies," I turned and looked him dead in the eyes, "I just watched men die. Men who were about to go home."

The next day, I took Lt. Crag Gies and Captain Denny Kramp over to where the attack occurred. Men were puking their guts out at the sight inside the orderly room where the CQ got his head blown off.

The men I saw running through the mortar rounds were dead men.

The smell of blood permeated the air.

This was not the kind of thing you would write a letter to your mother about.

WHERE'S THE PAPER CLIPS

ONE DAY WHILE WALKING over to the photo-lab – I learned how to develop my own film and make prints there – I spotted a General Officer and asked if I could take his picture. He went into a pose and that was the first image I had of General Sidney Berry.

I should point out that while I was the Battalion Stringer, I still had to perform duties for B Battery as well. So, on this day, as I began to walk back over to the unit, a pair of 122 rockets were fired at Camp Eagle and I had to run almost a quarter of a mile.

Just about where the armor vehicles were stored, the sounds of three 122s completely overshooting Camp Eagle came thundering overhead.

I'm running as fast as I can because – not because I'm scared of those very loud and noisy rounds but because I am the designated – Lt. Craig Gies – driver in charge of the interior perimeter guards.

I get within 250 feet and there he was honking at an empty hooch.

This rather funny humorous MASH movie image of why he didn't get out of the jeep and realize that I wasn't in the hooch, you idiot continued until I got within ear shot. "I'm right here sir."

"Why weren't you here?" he protested.

Sure, like I'm going to know when incoming rounds are going to come in. Schedule right in my pocket. I just got stupid this day and forgot to look.

So, he drives me around. A rather comical moment all things considered. And after he calms down.

"I don't think that is going to be the last of the

rounds we're going to see tonight."

"Why do you say that?"

We, let me see, I thought, that same little angle on my shoulder told me to stay in Da Nang on the afternoon of May 2nd and we got our entire unit wiped off the face of the earth on the morning of May 3rd so, yeah. It talks, and I listen.

"Just a gut feeling."

"I'm keeping the jeep in front of my hooch. If you're right, meet me there when it's all clear again."

So, I'm in my hooch, lying down in my cot with my TA 50 gear, flak jacket, and M-16 just waiting.

Charlie did me proud with a barrage of 122 rockets going everywhere sound like off the track freight trains.

It got quiet. A steely cold quiet when even the crickets and the frogs go dead.

I jumped up, went out the back door and started running towards the jeep.

You know that old saying, "it's the one you don't hear that kills you?"

Well, I'm here to tell you that ain't true. The first sound you hear you know the round is close. The red glare of the explosion followed by the blast concussion knocking you on your ass.

It hit right behind one of our Cobras roughly 200 feet away.

So, now, I'm sitting in the jeep honking the horn and Lt. Craig Gies comes cautiously out of his hooch with sleeping bag over his head.

"Damn, that was close. I wonder where it hit?"

"I can show ya, sir"

I did, and it was exactly where I saw it hit. While Joe Maxsom was shoveling dirt to contain the JP-4, our CO comes out to where we stood with all his combat gear on smiles, and asked where the round hit?"

We stare down at the hole; he throws down his

helmet in rage.

We sling loaded the damaged Cobra down to Red Beach.

Two days later, the CO invites me and Lt. Craig Gies into his office. It was time for me to say good-bye and go over to Headquarters and become the 4/77th stringer.

After the formalities, I went to salute and leave.

"Stay for a minute, Specialist Edwards. Want to show you what I have to put up with and besides you deserve seeing this."

You guys at A Battery who remember any of this ought to be laughing your asses off already.

So, he pulls out a cigar box. "A Troop sent this over to me."

Big letters "COBRA EMERGENCY REPAIR KIT"

Before he opens it up, I'm already laughing. Everyone looked at me wondering what I thought was so funny.

I was laughing because if I was an officer, I know what would be in that box.

And the boys over from A Battery didn't let me down.

Band Aids, rubber bands and I can't remember what the hell else was in that box because I and everyone else were laughing so hard – even the CO.

After we all gained a bit of composure, I said, "Sir, they seemed to have forgotten one thing?

"What's that?"

"Where's the paper clips?"

After all the laughter died down. I got serious.

"Sirs, it has truly been a pleasure working with and for you all.

"We've been through a hell of a lot together. From a unit pretty much destroyed to bouncing back and supporting the evacuation of Firebase Ripcord. Those are memories I will never forget."

I saluted, they saluted me back and I left the CO's office.

I was going to mention the Cobra Emergency Repair Kit at the end of my speech but that would have been over the top.

This night was the last time that Lt. Craig Gies and I would work together. My orders were officially in and I would have to move over to Battalion Headquarters.

Worked on a couple of articles that got published, went flying with the Battalion Commander and took more images of awards and decorations.

DAY I WENT TO LAW SCHOOL

ONE OF THE ENJOYABLE ASPECTS of being a stringer is that of finding articles and then convincing the powers that be to let you write the article based on hands on experience. One of those articles involved going over to the training area where many of the men and – I might add – women went to so they could understand better the various kinds of weapons we used.

In a couple of instances, we were able to fire some of these weapons. One of them was a LAW.

Weighing 2.37-kg (5.2 pounds) complete, the LAW was designed as a discard able one-man rocket launcher primarily for use as an anti-tank weapon. Its payload was a 5-pound High Explosive Anti-Tank (HEAT) warhead that could penetrate 14 inches of metal.

But we weren't using them for tanks, we were using them for bunkers, rock piles, holes in the ground and out houses that were to nasty to shit in.

One soldier could easily carry two – a total of ten extra pounds – and they were less bulky to carry than old school bazookas.

Another fact that made these "disposable" weapons attractive was – with their protective caps on both ends – they were airtight. With many situations where men had to traverse deep pockets of water, carrying these meant you also meant you were packing your own lightweight artillery with you.

When the LAW was handed to you, both the front and rear sights were folded down. Once you took both the front and back airtight covers off, and pulled up the sites, you could well figure out what you had to do next.

You had to guess the distances between you and the target. Mine was an APC about 250 meters out. You looked through the cross hairs in the back and lined up the number with the location of the target where you wanted the round to go.

Once you expanded the LAW, you owned it. Meaning, you had to fire the round. All you had to do is calmly fire the LAW down range.

Only problem with all of this is the fact that the firing button was covered with a piece of rubber that made it hard to fire. Because of this, you had to be steady and maintain sight of your intended target through pulling the trigger.

The LAW surprised me. It had about as much kick as my favorite weapon in Vietnam – the M79 grenade launcher. I aimed for the APC's top part of the track and hit it dead on. No real big explosion, just loud.

LAW school was over. With another believer in the LAW.

But I was on orders to go, so, I went. I think the chopper pilots were more scared about flying this mission than I or any of the other fellow soldiers. Landing on the back of a ship with the ship coming up and down in elevation of 15 feet isn't easy.

I can tell you that the ride to and from there was one of my better times based on the scenic views from 3,000 feet. And luckily for us, the landing went very well. We all jumped out and reported in.

HEADING TO THE HOSPITAL SHIP SANCTUARY

I WAS ORDERED to see an Ophthalmologist regarding my ability to perform the task of going on guard duty. And that meant going to the hospital ship Sanctuary. Short of going across the river between the main land of Vietnam and Eagle Beach on a landing craft, I hadn't been on any Navy ships. Based on this I had bitter sweet thoughts about going to a hospital ship just off the coast between Phu Bi and Da Nang.

So, I was told to report to the Medivac pad and fly out on the chopper at 9am.

The Sanctuary rotated between stations, such as Da Nang, Phu Bai, Chu Lai, and Dong Ha. The ship was close to Phu Bai on the day I was flown out to it.

Keep in mind that this ship was a Navy ship and its primary mission was to support the Marines. Not sure when that started including Army.

Anyway, you could feel the tension as we got close to the Sanctuary and asked for permission to land. And I think you can appreciate why. The ship was long meaning swells could bring the back end of the landing pad up and down by 10 feet without warning.

So, you didn't want to hover long above the platform.

Also, a bit unnerving is to have sailors crouched behind metal protection while holding fire extinguishers.

Since we didn't have any wounded, we were instructed to evac the chopper as swiftly as possible and do the same between the chopper and the ships entrance way.

For me, this experience was like a living oxymoron. Here I was on a hospital ship – with no combat related wounds, and who works for a Battalion whose sole purpose is to kill the enemy within 5 meters of our friendly forces – whose sole mission is to save lives.

I really felt out of place. Really, really, badly out of place.

A few moments later after sitting down an orderly comes along and asks why you are there and for papers.

About the same time you want to go to the bathroom, the alarms go off.

There is a rush of humanity to helipad.

It was like watching a war movie, only up close and personal. Like a tide going out, they come back in with a gurney, the ARVN officer and an American Officer talking to him in Vietnamese.

He died a few minutes later. They pulled the blood colored sheet over his head.

Later, an American soldier was wheel chaired past us, was taken down the hallway and was clearly drugged into senselessness stupor. A few minutes later coming from the direction where he was taken, wailing screams of pain and anguish sent chills down my spine. Like the pain I felt when I broke my arm in three different places.

I can only guess that he was told of the extent of his injuries. The half blown off foot was one of them.

There were a lot of women on that ship. Mostly nurses. For many of the dying soldiers, they were the last female voice they would ever hear. I can only imagine the horrors that they saw. The screams they heard. They were the true heroes of the war. They earned my respect that day.

After a while, we were told about the mess hall

Once in Nam, Always in Nam

(which I'm sure, that's not what it is called on a Navy ship or maybe it is) and that we would be processed through after that.

I don't think any of us were hungry after what we just went through. I just asked where I could go to the bathroom and grabbed some coffee at the mess hall.

When it was my time, an orderly came to me and told me to follow him. We walked through an open bay where men were recovering from their wounds. I saw men with chunks of skin missing and lots of bloody bandages. Many had smiles on their faces as they were glad to be alive – and probably still high from the drugs given to them to overcome their pain.

The ritual of seeing the Ophthalmologist was one I was familiar with. Eye drops, eye chart, which lens is better, this one or this one or this one?

So much a routine I could do it myself.

The Ophthalmologist comes in, flips through the charts and says, "I see you have amblyopic left eye.

"Yes, sir. I was diagnosed with it at the age of 6. When I get tired, it turns in. I've learned to live with it."

"Well, apparently, the Army hasn't. How well did you shoot in basic?"

"Sir, Sharpshooter with the M16, Marksman with the M14."

"Okay, so I'm going to approve you for guard duty. How would you like 20/50 in your left eye and learn how to strengthen your muscles, so it doesn't cross in?"

So, he ordered me a pair of prismatic lenses to help the two eyes work together and told me about some exercises I could do to strengthen the muscles.

Me, I didn't have any of these things going on. I simply needed conformation that I could shoot a rifle and kill if I had to.

This took all a few hours to complete. Also, I was given a new pair of glasses that forced my left eye to work with my right eye. And with a letter of approval, I was heading back to Camp Eagle with a different sense of reality on what giving your life for your country meant.

I was never so happy to get off that ship!

Guard duty consisted of a formation of the headquarters troops and B Battery troops and assignment of locations around the parameter. These locations had bunkers, starlight scopes, flares and what we called clackers – designed to generate a charge strong enough to fire off the caps in the claymore mines. There was a landline connected to each bunker.

"Hey, SP4 Edwards, you sure you got a firing pin in that gun of yours?"

I was still taking in my experience on the hospital ship.

I smiled and laughed with them. But was thinking: You pin heads have no idea what war really is.

Most of us who went to Nam pretty much figured out we weren't in front of our TVs watching John Wayne getting reincarnated, The Lieutenant or sergeant or, for that matter any show where the hero somehow manages to show up all clean, in one piece and just hankering for another peacemaker 12 noon showdown.

Took one visit to the hospital ship to slap me in the face with the facts of war. There is no glory in war. No turning off the TV here. You take a bullet or watch someone else get blown to pieces, your view on life chances almost immediately. And you remember it because it's the closest most brutal moment of your life. An event that makes sense to the meaning once in Nam, always in Nam. You're just on borrowed time after that.

HERE'S A LITTLE CS IN YOUR FACE

THE WIND WAS BLOWING from the southwest to the northeast. The B Battery troops were just north and east of my position. We were going to have a mad minute at 12 where we could fire everything we had – save the things like the claymore mines and the CS gas containers.

So, I put a 12-round clip into my rifle when it was time to free fire and aimed above the CS Gas container because I didn't want to hit it and fired away.

As it turned out, one of the phosphorous rounds caused the CS Gas to ignite and the cloud of CS gas slowly ventured over to my hecklers. The glasses as it turns out – while helping me force my eyes to work together, also caused my eyes to see the target lower than what it was.

So, while I thought the CS gas container was lower than it was, it was higher than what it was. So, I hit it with one of my rounds.

The landline was abuzz with pissed off coughing B Battery soldiers blaming me for their discomfort.

Well, how else would I prove to them that not only did I have a firing pin in my gun, but I could hit target 75 feet away with deadly accuracy.

Not to worry, they got back at me by firing a M-40 CS gas round at me using an M-709. It landed on the flight line and spun around 50 feet away.

As for me, I got called into the Cos office who threatened me with an Article 15 for the destruction of government property. But got told by him that I didn't have enough time left in Vietnam to do the paperwork

Richard T. Edwards

HEADING BACK TO OSAKA TO MEET THE 5ᵀᴴ DIMENSON

THIS TIME I HAD MY ACT TOGETHER. I got on the Bullet Train and headed directly down to Osaka, Japan.

One of the things you do best is not do the things that didn't work on the first trip but do the things that did.

Not only does it save you money, it saves you time and effort. Expo 70 – held in Suita, Osaka, Japan – ran from March 15 and September 13, 1970.

Planning a second trip there so that I could see the 5th Dimension perform at the Expo was pretty much a suicide mission. Why?

Well for one thing, the Expo was going to end one month later, summer crowds would increase the amount of people seeing the Expo and many tourists would be there from all over the world.

This meant that the Plaza International Hotel would be booked – as well as almost every other place.

Bottom line, either you had booked a hotel in advanced or, if you were an American from Vietnam, you slept on one of the park seats.

That was the picture you painted yourself into if you wanted to see the Expo and it wasn't pretty.

That is, unless you were me.

I had already been invited to stay with the folks at the Canadian Pavilion, so half the battle had been won.

Upon arrival at the Expo, I went over to the Canadian Pavilion and told my friend there was no place to stay and he knew that was true. So, he did good on his offer and I stayed the entire time over where the Canadians called their home away from home.

The place where they let me sleep was typical of Japanese style, sliding doors with a bed in the middle of the floor. I also noticed two jars with a white, creamy substance in them. Didn't take me long to add 2+2.

The only reason why they had invited me over was because they knew I would never take them up on it and this room was where they had bets going on how many girls they could have sex with while they were there. Basically, see which one could fill up the sperm jar the fastest.

I stopped thinking about it and went to sleep.

Next day, I walked over to the Expo and watched the 5th Dimension. They were fun to watch. But they made one mistake. I think they thought no one knew were the Plaza International was located because they kept mentioning that as the place where they were staying.

Next day, I was at the Plaza and sure enough the members of the group were sprinkled about.

I took pictures of Florence LaRue and Ron Townson outside and Lamonte McLemore inside and down stairs at a camera shop.

Marilyn McCoo was photographed at the end of the last show signing her name to the one of the show's posters. We had a conversation.

"That was a great show, much better than on Wednesday."

"Yes," she said laughing, "That's because we were half drunk."

I could tell she was from the east coast.

"So, where are you from?"

"Jersey"

"Me, too, Moorestown. But right now, I'm over in Vietnam"

"Well, if you're ever around in New Brunswick, give me a call."

I was starting to get used to invites.

I went outside to catch Billy Davis, Jr. He walked passed me.

"Mind if I take your picture?"

"No, no, no. No picture."

"Well that bites. A Vietnam solider can't get a photography of the famous Billy Davis Jr."

Billy turned around sharply – I thought he was going to hit me – and smiled.

I considered that mental picture to be the best I took.

I did get in a bit of trouble with the folks at the Canadian Pavilion when I spotted someone I knew sleeping on a park bench and suggested that he talk with my buddy. This was taken the wrong way. I never told my friend to ask them for a place to stay. I simply asked him to talk with my buddy in hopes they would know where he could stay.

Once cleared up, my buddy at the Canadian Pavilion settled down and helped me get a ride back up to Camp Zama.

Richard T. Edwards

GOING UP
TO THE DMZ

THERE WERE TIMES when I wasn't needed to take images of promotions, awards and decorations.

This allowed me to explore other story possibilities in and around the Hue/Phu Bai area other than just my unit and the 101st.

I was fascinated by all kinds of flying machines flown during the war.

There was one that was so quiet that when it flew without its anti-collision lights on you wouldn't even know it was there. Even with the anti-collision lights on, you couldn't hear it save the movement of air as it flew overhead.

Anyway, since I had all day to kill, I decided to go over to the Phu Bei airport and see if I couldn't take some images of the Air Force aircraft stationed there.

After taking a few images, I noticed a military version of a Cessna Sky Master. The Sky Master has two engines. One in the front and one in the rear. Because of this, you could be qualified as having a single engine FAA certification and filly it. The following is the O-2's specifications.

    General:
     Manufacturer: Cessna
     Base model: O-2
     Designation: O-2
     Version: A
     Nickname: Skymaster
     Designation System: U.S. Tri-Service
     Designation Period: 1962-Present
     Basic role: Observation

Specifications
  Length: 29' 9" 9.0 m
  Height: 9' 2" 2.7 m
  Wingspan: 38' 2" 11.6 m
  Wing area: 202.5 sq. ft. 18.8 sq. m
  Empty Weight: 2,705 lb. 1,226 kg
  Gross Weight: 4,630 lb. 2,099 kg
Propulsion
  No. of Engines: 2
  Power plant: Continental IO-360
  Horsepower (each): 210
Performance
  Range: 780 miles 1,256 km
  Cruise Speed: 196 mph 315 km/h 170 kt
  Max Speed: 206 mph 331 km/h 178 kt
  Ceiling: 19,300 ft.

Okay, it wasn't exactly an F-4 Phantom, but it would do.

Providing, of course, I could convince the pilot that this wasn't just a joy ride but a photo-feature in the making. Carrying bag with a nomex flight suit and gloves along with a Pentax made it much easier to convince the pilot that what I was wanting to do was the real thing and prove beneficial.

He asked me how close I had ever been to the DMZ and I told him up to Quang Tri. He laughed, "We're going to get a lot closer than that."

"The closer the better, Sir."

"You should be able to take a picture of that 30 by 50-foot flag at the border."

"I've never seen that photographed before, Sir."

He laughed, "You're going to see more than just a flag, I promise you that."

So, I pulled over my regular clothes my nomex flight suit, took off my helmet and replaced it with the flight helmet.

"You are still going to have to wear a flak jacket. Know how to fly?"

My heart raced, I had always wanted to fly a twin engine. Most of my stick time was in a single engine airplane.

"Yes Sir. I have 40 hours flying time and 12-hours' worth of training."

"Good to know."

Within minutes, the pilot was yelling "Clear" and the hefty baritone of the Continental engines roared into life. The pilot went through his checklist, made sure all the flight controls worked and got permission to take off.

Takeoff was smooth as glass. We gained altitude and headed north along the shoreline. My calculations on the flight time put us at 20 minutes away from the DMZ. We passed by Hue almost instantly, then we arrived parallel to Quang Tri in less than 15 minutes. Even when we flew low terrain flying – NAP of The Earth – it only took us 3 minutes to go the 11 of the 13 miles between Quang Tre and the DMZ.

I could see off the shoreline near the DMZ a Destroyer pumping in 5-inch shells into areas just below the DMZ.

"I'm not going to get any closer than this, so get your camera out and start shooting."

Which is exactly what I did. I only had one shot at getting that image of the 30x50 foot red flag with a gold star in the center.

Below the flagpole were the remains of at least three helicopters used by pilots who tried to make that flag theirs. Didn't quite work out for them.

Coming back, I took more pictures of the pilot and our trip back to Phu Bai. And 30 minutes later, we landed back at Phu Bai.

About a week later, the slides came back. Sure

enough, there was that 30x50 foot flag. Clear and sharp. After showing my images proudly to everyone at headquarters, I put those slides into slide protectors and left them in my desk drawer.

Two days later, I opened the locked drawer and found the image of the flag missing.

I'm not sure who got that image. My belief was our S-2 but it may as very well be our CSM. Whoever got it certainly wasn't going to let me know they did in this lifetime.

Luckily for me, I have a very good memory.

THE NIGHT *MASH* GOT TRASHED

THERE WAS A CHINOOK COMPANY – I think it was B Company, 159th Aviation Battalion but I'm not sure – directly across the street from Headquarters, 4/77th – I got assigned to it as the Battalion Stringer in the middle of July.

Sometime in August or September – I lost my mind by then – we wanted to watch MASH.

I mean WE ALL REALLY WANTED TO WATCH *MASH*.

So, there were in front of the silver screen, the projector almost as loud as the speakers. The smell of excitement in the air. Eyes focused on the screen.

On a planet known as Chinook field far, far away, the single whine of the small hydraulic turbine comes on line.

Eyes glued to the silver screen. Temperatures rising.

The twin engines come alive.

Whooping and hollering begins.

The blades increase in speed.

Naked, Naked ladies.

You hear the blades take to the task of lifting the Chinook into the air.

Then silence.

More naked, naked ladies.

KA WHAM!!

Listen, if was just a 122, we would have been really pissed and probably continued watching!

But NO metal was flying everywhere! whizzing by, hitting metal all around us. Oh, my god, this is it!

Some new way Charlie was coming at us with a new type of weapon none of us was yet familiar with and we were in the middle of it and had no idea where it came from.

125 men went from sex starved to craw daddy mode in an instant. The projector took a direct hit. Not clear if that was friend or foe.

It took what felt like ten minutes for all the metal to stop banging against things and three hours for us to wait for an all clear and realize it wasn't coming.

We all went to bed wondering what the heck happened.

Question, what does a Chinook look like landing upside down on top of where the rotor blades used to be?

Like a totally busted Chinook that landed upside down where the rotor blades used to be.

Sigh.

We never did finish *MASH*. So, I guess the knock, knock Chinook jokes was a satisfactory compensation.

BATES GETS COURT MARTIALED

YOU CAN PRETTY MUCH IMAGINE my surprise when I saw Bates walk out of the building where they court martialed soldiers with two armed guards. A civilian was taking pictures of Bates.

Clearly, Bates was getting court martialed.

But for what?

My journalist mind just had to know.

So, I walked up as close as I could and said, "Okay, what did you do?"

"Honestly, I don't remember. But from what they tell me it was bad, really bad."

"Did you kill someone?"

"No. But you'll read about it."

The guard got uncomfortable, so I stopped questioning. I said goodbye and walked away.

As it turns out, the night the 122mm rocket blew me backwards, Bates had been mixing liquor with LSD and his mind saw all the officers in the unit as little yellow men wanting to kill him.

So, he put an M-79 grenade launcher to the head of his CO and threatened to kill him and any other gook SOB who got in his way.

Of course, no one died except Bates' career.

Richard T. Edwards

RICHARD NIXON TOOK AWAY MY GTO

RICHARD NIXON SHORTENED MY TIME in Vietnam by almost 16 days. I was supposed to leave on the 12 of November. Instead, the date for leaving country was now the 25th of October. Unfortunately, typhoon Kate would have other plans. On October 25, the typhoon further weakened to a tropical storm just off the coast of Vietnam. Later that day, the system made its final landfall near Da Nang, Vietnam with winds of 100 km/h (65 mph). I didn't leave country until the 27th.

Anyway, I would be coming back to the states before turning 21. Meaning the $3300 I saved for the 1970 Plymouth GTO was a total waste of time because my parents would never co-sign for it. That wasn't speculation. That's what really happened.

Geis was gone, orders were cut, and I can thank him for the new MOS. A 71T20 Maintenance Data Specialist. And on top of all of that, I wasn't even going to a helicopter battalion. I was going to some wimp organization called the United State Army Intelligence Center and School. And that was located at Fort Holabird, Baltimore, MD.

Talk about adding insult to injury.

SERTS training moved up to Camp Evans and C Battery, 4th Battalion, 77th Field Artillery was responsible for putting on a show about what the AFA was about and what the Artillery Cobra can do. I needed some images of our Cobras in action and requested permission to ride front seat in the Cobra while the demonstration was taking place.

Richard T. Edwards

This got approved and I was flying in a "hot" Cobra taking pictures as we shot the mini gun, the 40mm grenade launcher and a dozen rockets.

These images were published in *Rendezvous with Destiny* magazine.

INCOMING IN AND INCOMING OUT

YOU GO TO PHU BI to process out a few days before you actually leave so, when the we arrived and got told you really weren't going anywhere for a few more days, you have some time to kill and – since nobody really cares at this point what you do – I decided to go back over to my old unit and say goodbye to some friends who were still there.

Big mistake.

While I did say goodbye, those freight train sounding 122's decided to do the same.

You know, it's very embarrassing to have to explain to a fresh young lieutenant who has less time in country than have in the chow line that you turned in your combat gear because you are already considered gone...and very funny, too.

The next night, with the wind howling and nothing was flying but the rain in my face, I walked about the hooch and reflected.

There were 5 new bees in the hooch who haven't gotten shot at yet or yelled at or worse had to drive shotgun on a trash truck. None have any idea what hell on earth is yet. But they were about to. I counted 12 this time. I hadn't a clue what they were firing currently, nor did I care. While they did walk towards my location, the 12 wasn't even close to home.

They woke up when the sirens went off.

"What was that, incoming."

"Yep," I said, "Twelve rounds of B-40 mortars and twelve hits nowhere near here. I'm going to bed because I'm tired and I have no combat gear anyway.

Neither do you, so I suggest you do the same."

They went back to sleep and so did I.

In the morning, I caught a C-130 from Phu Bi to Da Nang. This was where you changed clothes from combat fatigues to Class A uniform, were handed some orders to get on the freedom bird, converted the APC back to greenbacks and get you over to the tarmac where the 707s were being readied for the flight home.

Unfortunately, the holding area was backed up with three days' worth of flights. So, there was a bunch of really pissed off soldiers with ethnic issues. Bottom line: A bunch of war-tired soldiers who couldn't kill something were focused on each other.

I kept a low profile.

At 0500 hours on the morning of the 27th we ordered to group into single line formation according to the number of the airplane. Before chicken man woke up 500,000 Americans stationed in Vietnam, we were in the air coming home.

We went to an orphanage and I wrote a story about my experiences there. Aside from having to record the event, I also brought with me a movie screen and showed the children some movies.

This was published in Stars and Stripes and I read the article on the freedom plane coming home In Army Times. It was then that I realized writing and photography was something I was good at. Yes, I still had a lot of work ahead of me on the writing side of it. That would come with time. Nam was over. The memories have lasted a lifetime. But now, it was time to begin a new chapter. One that was filled with blank pages. I needed some new stories to tell.

COMING HOME

WHEN I CAME BACK from Vietnam in 1970, I was already on orders to be the United States Army Intelligence Center and School's Equipment and Records Specialist. It is much easier for United States Army Intelligence Center and School to be called USAICS.

I was about as far removed from combat and Army Aviation as you could possibly imagine.

I had no idea what a 71T20 was supposed to do much less how to do it.

By the time I felt comfortable with the new job, one of the senior staff members at USAICS told me that I was going to Fort Huachuca, AZ as part of the Advanced Party as USAICS was moving there

But I'm getting ahead of myself.

So, you get off the plane and your feet hit US soil for the first time in almost over a year. You're tired but you are glad you are home in one piece.

Your mind races.

350 days of listening to chicken man, incoming and outgoing rounds, of high pitched loud turbine engines, the popping of rotor blades competed with the smells of burning human waste, gunpowder, diesel fuel and JP4 turbine fuel.

The slightest sound of a backfire at this point would have had all of us ducking for cover.

You walk by them, long hairs and women whom which at this point where most of the living and the minority of the dead. We all wondering as we walked past them with no eye contact, if we couldn't just walk up to them and provide them with a condensed second of the hell we went through just to see them go crying to the mamas.

We go over to Fort Lewis, Washington, eat steak for breakfast. Listen to a West Point Colonel tell how appreciative the US Army was for our service. Then exchange combat fatigues for our Class As. I'm running around with orders for USAICS around the middle of November and have 2 rows of ribbons: National Defense Service Medal, Vietnam Service Medal, Vietnam Campaign Medal, an Army Accommodation Medal and a Bronze Star.

I should have also been awarded an Air Medal but that didn't happen.

I was also a Sharp Shooter with the M-14 and a Marksman with the M-16.

I was an E-4.

It was a long flight the next day between Seattle and Chicago. I spent most of the flight sleeping. When I was awake, two business men wanted to know if I had just got back from Vietnam and, I said yes. They thanked me for my service.

They had no idea who I was or what I did.

If they did, I would have been front-page news. The headlines would read SP4 in Vietnam single handedly rebuilds unit from an equipment and records administrative side in less than 60 days.

And it would be the truth because that was exactly what I did. The logistical side. I just didn't build the buildings.

From Chicago, we flew directly to Philadelphia and I went into Center City where I caught the bus home to Moorestown. It was Friday at 4:30pm when I knocked on the door and was greeted by my mother.

The rest of the two weeks were a blur. But the first Sunday, that was a different story. I went to Catholic Church at Our Lady of Good Counsel (OLGC) in full uniform. It would be the last time I would go to a

Once in Nam, Always in Nam

Catholic Church.

Anyway, once mass was done and I walked outside, I got swarmed by people I knew and didn't know. It was like finishing a lecture or a play and you were their hero.

It's never what you've done in the past that should be held in high esteem. It is the things you are going to do that is a true mark of a hero.

Anyway, the entire thing made me uncomfortable as I was asked questions I couldn't answer. But the one I tried my best to answer was what were all those ribbons I was wearing. And I suppose wearing them to civilians must have meant you did something special, that you're the Audie Murphy of Moorestown.

What are those two medals?" they asked, pointing to the Army Accommodation Medal and the Bronze Star.

"Oh," I said, "Those were given because I served on Vietnam." And they were. But that is not what they wanted to hear. So, they started walking away, unhappy with my response.

I almost felt sorry to disappoint.

Richard T. Edwards

LOOKING BACK THROUGH THE EYES OF A 68-YEAR-OLD

AS I GROW CLOSER TO FINISH adding the last chapters of this work, I find myself in a world where the men around me are in their 20s and 30s. They know little to nothing about Vietnam. They know we fought there, they know its someplace in Southeast Asia. But they don't know the stories.

Those who do have been fed spit-shinned stories with a thread of truth and a lot of vague, distorted fluff.

No, I didn't die. No, I didn't kill anyone. No, I wasn't a pilot. And more importantly, no, I didn't hate the Vietnamese.

Truth stings like the stench of human waste mixed with kerosene burning nearby and filling your nostrils with the acrid smell. You cannot take back anything. You cannot bring back the dead or remove senses experiences, the humiliation or the degradation a Vietnam Veteran went through.

Those things got buried, like a dog buries a bone in the back yard, in the back of your mind. Either that or it drove you crazy with pain and sorrow.

It is my hopes through all of this to paint a truer picture of the life and times of a soldier who felt betrayed by a system with no conscious. A system above the law. A system that has, is, and will be doing what it pleases without retort.

Some of the articles here seem rude and crude. I make no apologies. There were times when rude and crude gets the job done.

Richard T. Edwards

I pray that all of you – both Vietnam Veterans, their spouses and their children – both find something here worth reading and leave my world I've painted for you with this:

We may have died young, but we lived with the strength of steel. We may have come back in various percentages of complete body and mental faculties, but the strength of our soul triumphs.

As for me, I may be getting old, but I ain't dead yet.

My last thought here. The other day my younger brother equated me as being older than dirt. I retorted with, older than dirt implies I'm heading in the direction of the grave. Call me younger than sunshine.

STUFF THAT JUST DOESN'T FIT ELSEWHERE

Richard T. Edwards

THE BREAKFAST CLUB

TO: General William Childs Westmoreland

From: Everyone who was between 19 and 24 and was E-1 to E-5

Dear Sir:

It has come to our attention that you may be concerned and confused as to why we smoke weed, overdose on beer, run around topless in broad day light and pretty much question every order someone who 10 years is older or of higher rank than ourselves shoves under our noses.

While it is true we are ornery, hate wearing a military uniform, love having a good time, go to church, have this insatiable desire to left alone and have sexual thoughts about every seven minutes, we still get things done.

We come to you in all shapes and sizes, all colors of skin, all levels of education. We are writers, poets and artists, we have PhDs, we have GT scores from 60 to 150, we love listening to Credence Clearwater Revival and we don't want to be here.

But we are, and we'll do our best to make the time go away as quickly as possible.

I'm sure from your perspective, this all sounds horrible. The truth does have a way of slapping you around like finding a live cobra snake in your bed.

Based on your impressive long life as a well-disciplined officer and leader, you've seen your fair share of us and know we either get out and get just as disciplined as you over time or we stay in and join your flock.

There's just so many of us now all in one spot and we're just about the unruliest lot you've ever seen in your life.

You can blame it on the school system. They taught us we had the right as Americans to be individuals.

They didn't teach us how to be soldiers.

Welcome to Vietnam!

Sir, unless you have a problem with this, we do burn your human waste, we fill your sand bags, we paint your rocks, we peal your potatoes, we go on guard duty, we get shot at, we watch men die, we have no idea why the enemy loves firing 122mm rockets at us, know when women are in the immediate vicinity, we brush our teeth and swallow a pill the size of a 30 odd 6 bullet.

Could you get rid of chicken man? Guess that's too much to ask.

We make sure the NVA doesn't tear us a new asshole, go on patrol, watch other friends die or are so mangled they wish they had, and get fired at by our own men and helicopters.

Pardon my French, sir, who was the freaking idiot who thought clean pressed fatigues, spit shined shoes, and polished brass in a combat zone?

Does that have anything to do with our ability to kill the little yellow man?

Why do we use choppers whose rotor blades can be heard coming as far as 5 miles away think that's the element of surprise?

Its surprises, us sir, that we have enough common sense to realize you don't ever compromise your position as that is the element of surprise. And always, always get the first punch in. We learned that from our street fighting days.

You should know that based on our own intelligence gathering process that you are underestimating the intelligence of your enemy as they are constantly listening to our radio chatter and the civilians working on post are constantly ratting us out.

What do we know?

We love loud music, wild people like the Rolling Stones and have people with emotional issues – they like Simon and Garfunkel.

Despite all the crap about segregation, the blacks sleep with the blacks, the Mexicans with the Mexicans, the Puerto Ricans with the Puerto Ricans, the refers with the refers, the mafia with the mafia, the alcoholics with the alcoholics and the undecided with the undecided.

Did I bother to mention this was by their choice and one us white boys forced on them.

Only ones left are.... this may come as a shock to you ... the gays.

Is it true that the government was conducting genetic experiments with babies born in 1949?

We got some wide hipped guys with thin waists running around here with no hair on their chest and never shave...just asking.

We bleed like you, too. We've got cuts, bruises, and body parts missing. We breathe oxygen. We party hard and tell you to take your Army system and tell you to shove it up your ass.

That probably gets us into more hot water than anything else. Point is, we ain't your boy scouts and this ain't no jamboree.

We also die hard and, in the process, make our mothers weep, or friends cry and our world safer.

Isn't that what you wanted from us?

Hand me a gun, have the enemy come at me, he's going to drop like a turkey.

Speaking of which, why is it that every patrol I go on, it's the tallest guy that gets the job of carrying the radio?

You need to make a policy that the smallest guy – about the size of boots and helmet on top – should have

Richard T. Edwards

to carry the radio.

You all take us too seriously, we're just a bunch of RA's and US's that either were too stupid to read the fine print or got drafted. We're just as confused as you are about us as we are about ourselves.

By the time you read this, some of us will be in body bags, some of us will be wounded in action, some of will be walking dead and die before our time from agent orange.

And some of us will live to tell our stories to our generation, our children's and even some of theirs.

We are your rag tags, you slackers, your goof balls and your heroes. And when it comes time to work as a team, no matter what hooch we come out of, sometimes kicking and screaming, we do work as a team without thinking of the consequences.

We get it done.

Well that pretty much sums up what I wanted to say.

Sincerely yours,

The Breakfast Club

WARRANT OFFICER FRED CAPPO

BECAUSE I WAS AN E-3 at the time – a/k/a enlisted – and, unlike years later, when General Officers knew me personally – we were the low class, low-life's and they were the elite.

That wasn't the case with Denny Kramp, Lt. Craig Gies, and Fredrick Cappo. These gentlemen made me feel good, made me feel like I was doing something I could be proud of.

Now, Cappo could have easily been shot down himself that day and killed. Instead, he landed beside the crippled Cobra and flew to two pilots out on his rocket pods and skids.

This man should have been given the Medal of Honor. Instead, he got a Silver Cross. Why? Because like me, he didn't play by the book.

For all the work I did for my unit, for all the things I did for them above and beyond, nothing, nada, zilch was award to me.

No Air Medal, nothing. All I got from Vietnam was an ARCOM and a Bronze Star. Standard issue of you kept your nose clean.

But this is Fred's story.

This was the first time – and not the last – that Frederick Cappo would show up on my radio performing gutsy move. An example of this was when he was flying by a mountain we called nu e ka. He observed some 122mm rockets being fired from that mountain and alerted Camp Eagle that some enemy rockets were launched.

No telling how many lives were saved because he

reacted the way he did. But he didn't stop there. He fired all his 2.75-inch rockets at the location where those 122mm rockets were being fired and probably stopped more 122mm rockets from being fired at us.

What did he get for his efforts? A letter of reprimand stating that firing rockets at a target without first making sure the area was cleared of friendly forces was in violation of standard rules of engagement.

What very few people knew – and the by the book officers were totally clueless – was those 122mm rockets that Fred called in were marked for civilian targets on the other side of Camp Eagle. So, while we heard the sirens go off that we were under attack had either hit or were about to, the first volley never hit Camp Eagle at all.

It is the belief of this writer that because Fred did what he did stopped the NVA from firing a dozen or more of these rockets. Not only at us but at other civilian targets. Later, that night, additional 122mm rockets were fired at civilian targets and a single 122mm rocket was launched hitting right behind one of our AH-1G Cobras. The force of the explosion pushed me backwards as I watched it hit while trying to beat Lt. Craig Gies to a jeep.

Fred was also a friend. When I wanted to learn more about how to take pictures, he provided me with a book on how to use the Ashi Pentax.

I didn't return the book back to him until 1975 when we were both assigned to the 2/17th Cavalry. I also gave him my Cobra Tie which was presented to me by Bell Helicopter Textron as a thank you for all the publicity I created promoting the use of the TOW Cobra in Germany.

Fred, my hat is off to you Sir for being the Maverick you were.

STARLIGHT, STAR BRIGHT, TELL ME THERE AIN'T NO CHARLIE CONG IN MY WIRES TONIGHT

MOTTO, "Keep it clean and the batteries fresh, a starlight scope can save your life."

Well, it's hard to keep a starlight scope clean since the ones we got out on outside parameter guard duty never seemed to work as promised. And, of course, it would have been nice, to know how to use them before we went out on guard duty.

The one I had in Nam wasn't mounted on a rifle; in fact, it wasn't mounted on anything.

There was a good reason for this. It wasn't the easiest accessory to mount on a rifle.

Furthermore, with less than a few seconds between you a crazed enemy soldier hell bent on ripping you a new asshole, you don't have the luxury of securing it to a rifle, aligning it with the barrel of your gun and adjusting the forward magnification and back focusing lens.

The starlight scope was a piece of equipment a sniper would love and a guard on guard duty would hate.

However, that is not to say the scope didn't have is place on guard duty. The idea was to focus the scope between 50 and 100 feet out and then scan that area for possible movement. At the first sight of any movement, hand flares would be popped, making the scope useless anyway, and if there really was an enemy trying to turn our claymores on us, well, he'd be pushing up rice in his rice paddies.

Starlight scopes work off the premise that a certain amount of ambient light is generated from the stars and the moon and reflects off objects as it normally does in daylight. Problem is, there isn't enough of the light normally at night to see much of anything with the naked eye.

The starlight scope takes that ambient light and intensifies it. It is this intensified light that is projected on the back eyepiece that a soldier would see and could use to discern between nothing and an enemy soldier.

Again, training was an issue here. How can you know you were looking at an enemy soldier if you weren't trained to know what to look for?

All too often, what a guard on duty really saw wasn't a man at all but a monkey. Which meant, we spent a lot of time and sent ammo on monkeys and not on enemy soldiers.

MUD, MUD, GLORIOUS MUD

OKAY, IT MIGHT NOT be so glorious. But it was mud.

A glorious brick red clay like mud.

Did you know that during the monsoon season all the trenches fill up with mud?

Now, for some of you, it's just mud. A pain in the butt to remove from boots and you're never quite sure just how deep the mud is as everything around a drainage ditch possesses the same color and consistency.

So, this brings us to a quagmire (pardon the pun), what does a mud bather like myself do when the monsoons come along and provide ample places where you can wallow in the mire and release some sexual tension?

NOT GET NAKED AND DIVE RIGHT IN!!

That's for sure.

But it was mud.

Did I say I happen to like mud baths? Sorry if I'm repeating myself. I'm just a stick in the mud and stuck on the subject.

Nothing like one. Thick, creamy and cleans your pores.

Only problem, you are supposed to be a professional in a military uniform. Just try sneaking out at night and going to one. Some frag crazed refer head might just mistake your muddy body for being a satchel carrying Charlie Cong wanting to drop his load on their weed smelling drainage culvert.

"Sorry, ma am, but your son was found naked covered in clay with a smile on his face. But shot dead by a fellow soldier who thought he was an enemy soldier."

What a hell of an epitaph: "Here lies Richard Edwards with a bullet through his heart. Found, naked, covered in mud in a drainage ditch. RIP."

Of course, the opposite could have happened. I could have fantasized about being RAMBO and was about to do battle with 50 Charlie Cong and been caught by an officer.

Stars and Stripes would have had a field day with it: Soldier found naked covered in clay.

A soldier from the 101st Airborne Division Air Mobile was reported to have this crazed look on his face and was carrying nitroglycerin charged arrows with a compound bow.

He's being charged with the destruction of government property.

However, he will probably get out of the service with a general court martial and be required to get psychiatric care.

Plus, you really didn't know what might be in that mud. Dog turds, human waste, leaches, pesticides, and all sorts of stuff that could kill you later could have been in that stuff.

The point is, no matter how much the urge to do something as insanely fun as mud bathing is, while the red clay was inviting, it wasn't something you would do if you wanted to live and not die slowly over the next 60 years of your life.

But it was mud

THE DAY MEN WERE OVERCOME BY A FORCE THAT WON THEIR HEARTS

I CAN'T REMEMBER my exact words I wrote. All I knew was the article was published in Screaming Eagle, Stars and Stripes and Army Times. I couldn't pen it because I also included myself in the story with quotes. Below, is the closest I'm going to come to the original article:

Soldiers of the 4th Battalion, 77th Field Artillery knew they were outnumbered, even though they were armed to the teeth with plenty of delicious ammo.

The opposing forces knew just where they were the weakest. The Nuoc Ngot Orphanage children's' eyes glued on the bulging pockets and the enticing scent of sweets motivated them into action. The attack was on! It was all over before it got started. Not a drop of blood was shed. But in the end, a few tears were.

The air was filled with the screams of glee as the soldiers opened their pockets and started pulling out from their ammo pockets bar after bar of Hershey's chocolate.

"These children need our help," said Sp4 Harold Roberts, a Cobra crew chief for B Battery, 4th Battalion, 77th Artillery, 101st Airborne Division (Air Mobile), from Spokane, WA.

"They didn't choose to be here. They can't feed themselves. They can't defend themselves.

"They are as human as you and me, and we're here

to show our support."

The 101st Airborne (Air Mobile) has been supporting Nuoc Ngot Orphanage in Hue for the past three years. In other words, since the unit arrived in the area.

Once a month a unit from the 101st Airborne Division (Air Mobile) comes to the orphanage to show support; they bring food, clothing and money. They also provide the children with some laughs and good times.

In a place where the world saw Hue on TV as a place where the NVA fought our military during the TET offensive, it's hard to believe a year and a half later, that same city is the refuge for orphaned children from all walks of life.

The 4th Battalion, 77th Field Artillery brought with them some special treats for the children as Sergeant Franklin Spencer, A Battery, 77th Field Artillery, from Chicago, IL, had the children gather around him for 30-minutes' worth of magic tricks.

This gave SP4 Richard Edwards, B Battery, 4th Battalion, 77th Field Artillery, from Moorestown, NJ, time to set up the projector, thread the film through it and set up the portable projector screen.

"It was amazing to me to see 30 children of all ages sitting on the ground and spell bound while watching Tweedy-bird cartoons on the silver screen.

"I only wish I could have brought more cartoons for them as they seemed to enjoy them. They may not have known English that well, but they knew when to laugh at.

"Just to see that sparkle in their eyes, the smiles on their face was enough to know the extra effort to bring the projector, films and projector screen to the orphanage was well worth it and rewarding."

With everything packed in that was going back to

Once in Nam, Always in Nam

Camp Eagle, the soldiers of the 4th Battalion, 77th Field Artillery, gave each child a hug, handed each another Hershey bar said goodbye to the children of the Nuoc Ngot Orphanage, got back into their vehicles and started their trek back to Camp Eagle.

The men's mood had changed. Somewhere quiet, some reflective, a few had tears rolling down their cheeks of otherwise hardnosed faces. All that day realized those children had won their hearts with the innocence of their smiles.

On the "freedom bird" flight home, I read this story published in Army Times on October 27, 1970. I rolled up into a ball beside the window and felt the tears of pride weld up in my eyes. I was, in fact, nothing like my father. I had flown with the eagles.

I fell asleep with those thoughts and wondered how I would write the next chapter of my life. Little did I know, it was about to come to me in buckets.

Richard T. Edwards

I AM USELESS WITHOUT MY P-38

IT WASN'T A WWII twin-engine aircraft known as a P-38. It wasn't the sexiest. It was small, light and portable and when you wanted to open a can in a C-Ration box of food, this tiny piece of equipment was the way you did it.

Developed in just 30 days during the Summer of 1942 by the Subsistence Research Laboratory in Chicago, this small but handy two-piece field pocket can opener saw more war time than three generations of men.

You simply unfolded the blade from the main piece and placed it on the edge of the can so that the blade could puncture the can along the rim. The groove used the rim of the can and allowed the solider to easily penetrate the can with little effort.

Once you got the can started, pulling the can opener back to where the last incision stopped and repeating the ratcheting action is how you got the job done.

A few problems were never considered.

First, No P-38 had ever been made for a left-handed person. Meaning you had to open cans with your right hand.

Second, having a lose blade that flies open while attached to the dog tag chain could cause bodily harm.

Third, wives are not impressed with us opening cans at home with one. Post Nam dependencies on such equipment may help cut costs on electricity. But an electric can opener can open three cans of the same size in the same amount of time it takes you to do one.

Therefore, doing this more than once can cause a woman to swing a baseball bat at one's head or worse the P-38 itself vaporizes. I know, it has happened to me!

Since the P-38 is light and easy to hide, find such a place and leave it there. Instead of a baseball bat, when there is no electricity goes out and that can opener save the day, you might get something else.

C-RATIONS SOCIALIZATION IN A BOX

IF THERE WAS ANY ONE THING that would get us together in Vietnam every time, it was when we were given C-Rations.

Why was that the case?

Because C-Rations had things in them that you could barter with. You would have a small bag in each with Chiclets, salt, pepper, sugar, four cigarettes, matches and toilet paper. That you got in every C-Ration.

Personally, the John Wayne candy bars my favorite. The can of Quartered Pears, or Fruit Cocktail was next Peanut butter and cheese spread eaten using the plastic spoon also worked for me.

Never did care about the ham and eggs.

Anyway, there were various types of C rations you got in a box of 12 but you weren't sure what you were getting until you opened the individual units up. But you were sure of one thing. You had something someone else wanted and you wanted someone else didn't want. And when you didn't smoke cigarettes, well, you could almost get anything you wanted.

Richard T. Edwards

FSANGC RAIDS

MY EXPERIENCES IN VIETNAM would not be complete without a few encounters with melodrama. I mean, after all, why would you want to writer about Vietnam if everything you did was routine, on the up and up and didn't add a single line to someone else's day of infamy?

So, what does FSANGC stand for? Find, Steal and Not Get Caught.

Wait, wait, before you go sigh and turn me off, we had perfectly good reasons to want to perform these mini raids. They just wouldn't hold up in a court of law.

But then our primary targets weren't exactly maintaining straight ledgers either.

Suppose, for example, you were looking for the newer, thicker skid pads for your 12 AH-1G Cobras and knew a set – just one set, mind you – would mean the difference between having 4 sections up instead of three.

So, you go to your parts manual, get the part number, fill out the request card and drive over to the helicopter parts supply center. You just spent an hour doing all of this and the E-6 behind the desk has got an attitude problem, sizes you up and tells you he's fresh out.

Now, as a SP-4, you're not exactly in the driver's seat to tell this dip shit to get off his dead ass and look at his parts list to see if the part truly does or doesn't exist.

And when you can see the parts just feet away from you and you have a Cobra down because of this … it's time for Batman and Robin to appear in the raw black ink of a red dust filled night.

It was time to give that E-6 and attitude adjustment.

It was time for a FSANGC raid.

Understand we really weren't trying to do anything legal. Technically, we were just trying to keep an Aviation unit flying and combat ready. So, consider the following peeves. One, all parts supply centers had excess parts on hand for their local units. Even when a Red Ball order – one that is of the highest priority and requires immediate attention – comes in, the E-6 has the right to not take his last one off the shelf.

And when I'm looking right at those skid pads and its June 18th when we were flying every Cobra that was able to fly to support our soldiers from being massacred up at Fire base Ripcord, I'm sorry if stealing those pads could land me in jail, I'm going to get those pads and I'm going to make damn sure they're on that Cobra no later than the dawn of the next day.

So, Lt Geis and I went over to the same supply center and I dropped him off on the side of the building. We had done this twice before, so I was well versed on what I was supposed to do next.

I walk in the supply center and said, "I'm back!"

"Okay, what do you want this time?"

"Grab some coffee and just chit chat about Ripcord."

"Ripcord?? Yeah, every one's talking about Ripcord like it's some big deal."

"I know, it's horrible. Chinook goes down, the fire base is pretty much destroyed, and they have to live in the CS gas while constantly getting shelled by Viet Cong mortars." I said as a matter of fact.

About then, Lt. Gies slips producing a horrendous clamor the dead would have been woken up by.

"What was that?" asked one of the parts clerk to the other.

"Well, it wasn't incoming," I suggested, "So maybe the wind knocked something down."

Okay, so this wasn't working. So, I did something I used to do as a kid.

"So, here's the real reason why I'm here tonight. And hear me out before you say no, okay?"

They were both willing to listen. That was a good thing.

"I really came down here for one thing. Now, you can tell me no. But I can see what I need from here. So, I know you have the part.

"I could go through normal channels and get those Cobra skid pads by placing the order with you for them in three days. The men up at Ripcord don't have three days to wait for additional support from us or for that matter, from anyone else.

"So yeah, you can tell me you're out. But I'm going to tell you that without them, two Cobras won't be flying tomorrow and when you're flying 24-hour missions 7 days a week, these additional Cobras will become instrumental in saving the lives of our fellow soldiers.

"So, think about the decision you're about to make and realize that part isn't just a part, it represents the loss of American lives."

I got two pairs of skid pads, tied them to the back of my jeep and picked up Lt. Gies near the corner of the building.

"Sir, are you alright?"

"I'm fine, Dick. Jesus Christ, how did you pull that one off?"

"Just told them the truth, Sir.

"Our Cobras are saving lives up on Ripcord. Having two down due to skid pads would mean the loss of more American lives. I'm sure, they didn't want that kind of guilt on their conscious."

Our 4 sections continued to fly and support the efforts to soften up enemy strong holds. When you're out numbered 40 to one, our Cobras played a vital role. The following is from the After-Action Report from Firebase Ripcord:

Heavy 12.7mm anti-aircraft fire was directed against the aircraft flying into the firebase.

Air, artillery, and ARA destroyed several enemy mortars and 12.7mm machine guns.

In addition, numerous enemy driven into the open by CS were killed by air, artillery, and ARA.

Sometimes, just explaining the impact of a decision can make all the difference.

We never did another FSANGC raid again.

FICTION AND BITS & PIECES OF FICTION

AS I HAMMER THIS WORK into something worthy of your time to read, I discovered that I had some work that was totally made up.

By totally made up, I mean while parts of this are true, the rest of it is pure fiction.

My problem is, when I wrote them, they seemed longer on a blog then they do write out here in manuscript format.

Nevertheless, while they are short, I felt that they should be added simply because they are good reads. Sometimes, it is best to have less and say more than having more and saying less.

One of the fiction pieces: Roll on brother, roll on; was written before I found out that a pilot was well known for doing exactly that.

But that's not the first time I had my fiction weave itself into a real-world reality. I had a story accepted in IRON HORSE and it dealt with the use of a helicopter for a bank heist at Fort Polk, Louisiana. As it turned out, when we are about to publish the work, an actual heist did happen, and the criminals used an Army Huey as their get away vehicle. So, I had to rewrite the article to use something else other than a bank heist and a helicopter to get the work published.

Life, indeed, can be stranger than fiction.

With that said, I hope you enjoy the work as much as I enjoyed making it up.

Richard T. Edwards

ROLL ON, BROTHER, ROLL ON

THE AIR IS COLD, but the sky is hot with the hammer of rotor blades. Pilot in the front says, "Give them all you got, boys."

We dive to towards the ground and sink our lead into the Hot LZ We're spitting support and giving it out best shot.

Wild-eyed men sitting around us wonder if we've gone mad. And I'm thinking, Welcome to Nan.

Popping ammo boxes left and right, we're yelling to them to get out and stay low. Plenty of brush out there. And if they heard us, they'll live the drop off.

Our tracers paint a line to the edge of the perimeter and then left and right.

We lift away amidst the rain of enemy fire and watch the Cobras come down from the sky in a furious roar follow those tracers and wax the area with strafing and 2.75-inch rocket pounding so viciously well that at 500-foot-long, 2-foot-wide newly formed creek bed.

We're clear of the enemy fire. But then look at each other confused, "Okay, sir, what are we doing?"

"Playing medevac, one of ours took a round in the leg. He'll bleed out before a real one gets here."

Ground chatter gets crazy. Seems like when heaven opens its doors, bravery doesn't have to knock.

F-4s were our angles this day as they filled that creek bed with napalm. We could feel the heat from left and right. Hear Charlie Cong's screams into vaporization.

Karama is a bitch.

The extraction took 10 seconds. Lying him down and raising his leg, my belt just above the wound helped to slow the bleeding. But his heart was pounding too hard. Field expediency took care of that.

The pilots looked back and laughed. "Well that's one way to get it done."

"Figured I didn't have to ask permission, sir"

"For what, we didn't see anything."

The pilots switched radio channels. Just off the coast of Phu Bai was a white ship with a red cross on it.

"Sanctuary, this is hotel one nine six seven. We have a wounded soldier with a whole through his main artery in his leg. We're running low on fuel."

Do you know that ship turned and gave us a straight in approach to the back of the ship? And in less than five minutes we landed, the gurney was pulled over, and the wounded unconscious solder left on the gurney, and we were gone.

Few months later, I'm polishing up the Plexiglas on my bird and I see his reflection, I turned around.

"Can I help you, Sir?"

"You've got a hell of a left hook, Sergeant."

I chucked nervously, "That's what they tell me, Sir"

I hit a Captain? Damn, I should have hit him harder.

"They tell me that punch saved my life. They also told me that your belt also helped to stop the bleeding. So, I'm writing you up. Not for assaulting an officer, but for an act of bravery."

"Sir, I was just trying to help another American solder from being sent home in a body bag."

"I understand, but the way I see it, if I don't write you up, you'll never remember my name and I want you to remember my name."

I said, "yes, sir".

We saluted each other. As he walked away, "Sir, how did you find me?"

"It was on your belt. A name I will never forget."

Thirty years later, I'm flipping through my Facebook page and there he was. A West Point retired Four Star and he's speaking to a West Point graduating class. I click on the link.

He starts with, "You may, as I have had to do, put men into harm's way. Honor these men with as much respect and dignity as you expect them to respect the orders you give.

"And there may be times in your career when you find yourself totally depending upon them who hold the balance of life or death in their hands. Karama is unyielding.

"When we went into the field in Vietnam, we officers knew our rank was what the North Vietnamese were trained to look for, so it came off during insertions.

"I took a round out there. Went clean through my leg but nicked an artery. Two brave pilots, a door gunner and a crew chief by the name of Sergeant Billy Martin decided that I was going to bleed out."

About that time, in the kitchen the plate drops by my wife who thought I was full of it when I'd tell her about the story.

"Under the protection of F-4s hitting the edges of the enemy perimeter with napalm, they come in, pick me up. The crew chief pulled out a rolled-up belt he had in one of the pouches he was carrying and put it above the wound. He made sure I was flat on my back and raised my leg.

"He checked my pulse, smiled down at me and with a mean left hook, he knocked out. Plum out of my misery. Hell, I didn't remember a thing past that until after surgery. That was the meanest left hook that ever took."

After the laughter. The General continued.

"Well, thanks to his belt, I knew where to find him. At first, I think he thought I was going to throw the book at him. Write him up for hitting an officer. But I was there to think him for saving my life. Told him I was going to write him up for an act of heroism.

"I never did. I don't think that was what he wanted. In fact, I don't think any of the enlisted soldiers really want to have to explain to others the things that they did that measure up to an act of bravery.

"What I believe young solders want it to go home in one piece both mentally and physically. And in Vietnam, I think we were too brazen to think of our young enlisted soldiers as anything but a human machine being told what to do and how to do it.

"So, today, I'm ending this with a warning. You hold the rank of an officer and in battle, you hold your life in the hands of our enlisted soldiers. Why should they honor you with respect if you don't honor them with yours? These are men and not machines.

"As for me, I am forever in debt to the man who saved my life by knocking me out with meanest left hook that ever took.

"Thank you for your time, may god be with you all."

Wife whispers, "That was really you," with a newfound air of respect.

And all I could think about is his eyes staring through the camera at me while saluting the class and what I wanted to say back to him in person, "roll on brother, roll on."

A HELL OF A STORY

I HAD JUST COME DOWN from a seven-minute sensuality contest with one of the prettiest dames I had ever laid eyes on. Skin soft. Mounds firm. Stomach flat, and a racy set of legs that delivered what the rest promised.

There was something of intimacy and sadness in those crystal blue eyes that said more about this woman's angel face and long black hair. She was like a lonely mare whose time had passed but still looked as good to me as the mare looked to a stallion.

The cool breeze battled against the heated stench being radiated off the sun-cooked cement. If felt good against a sweaty skin. I took in a deep breath of the heat, slid out the pack of Cool Super Longs, pooped open the box and pulled out the menthol laced pipe tobacco smelling cancer stick.

Once in my mouth, I turned against the wind, cupped the lighter with my hand and dipped the tip into the gold tipped flame. I breathed in. Nothing like having menthol in your lungs after a woman treats you to her honey scented warmth.

I looked up; he was still doing a long circle to my right. Tall and built like a well-seasoned Green Beret.

He came over to me. His face was hard with a hint of a scar on his face where a steely knife from a frenzied assailant tried for the jugular but was to dead to strike true.

"Can I buy a cigarette from you?" he asked in a voice that didn't match his body.

"Why don't I just give you one instead? You don't

mind if its menthol?"

The big man shook his head. I whipped open the pack and handed him one.

"Need a light?

Again, big man shook his head.

He walked away a few lights down, pushed his back against the pole and pulled out what I expected to see. It was Nam bought. The lighter was a flip open with your thumb liquid filled type. The sharp spring action of the top made that familiar pop the top sound and the engravings on it looked like the work I had seen in Saigon.

I could smell her before I heard her. Had I not, at the very least, she would have a black eye. She walked like the breeze.

"See you've met my brother?"

"Your brother," I said incredulously.

"Okay, he's actually not my brother. But stepbrother. Never been the same since Vietnam. Used to be fun, loving and easy going. They turned him into a cold, shell of a man who could cut you up into pieces and not miss a good night's sleep," she said in a dry matter of fact way.

"So why do you..."

She put her finger over my lips and told me to not ask with those story line eyes of hers.

"He makes me feel safe. That's all you need to know...that and the fact that your cools are in his pocket.

"Don't go their soldier boy," she warned softly. "Let him be."

She was of course right. His reaction time was lightning fast as I never did see the lighter light the cigarette or go back into his pocket.

"Besides, I rather enjoyed you," she said in a way that I knew was truthful. "I haven't been that aggressively plowed into since my dead husband did me like that."

"Do you know, for such a beautiful woman, you sure have a 'to the point' way with words."

"Well, when you were married to a Green Beret, speak your mind and get to the point.

"So, I'll get to mine. Charles died near Kea Sanh during Lam Son 719. Got killed by friendly fire.

Little bit of me died with him. The part where I would never marry another man."

She paused for a moment, pulled out a pack of Marlboro Lights and handed me two. I put one between my head and my right ear. She lights hers and then lit mine.

"Not Menthol but better than trying to tackle that bear over there." she advised.

"You're a reporter, aren't you?" she asked without expecting an answer.

"Is that painted on my butt somewhere," I asked.

"No, but the fact that you were in Vietnam is with that tattoo on your arm. And a lefty, no less."

"Guilty as charged," I said my body going through the motions of surrendering to her.

That made her laugh. The chuckle wavering through her as her long hair almost caught fire being blown in her face, she pulled her hair back behind her head and tied it back with a rubber band.

"Tell you what, you listen to a story about that man two light poles up and I treat you to seconds.

"Deal?"

How could I refuse?

"Deal."

"Then speak softly as I am and so he can't hear you, Okay?"

"Okay" I said in a softer, quieter tone.

"That man over there is Robert Crowley..."

Richard T. Edwards

"Wait a minute, THE Lieutenant Colonel Robert Crowley???"

"One in the same."

"I did a piece on him when I was in Saigon. He served 5 tours in Nam from 68 to 72."

"Yes, and he won the Congressional Medal of Honor..."

"And then proceeded to TKO his commanding officer. Which of course destroyed his career in the military." I said with respect and awe. "But no one knows why he decked the Colonel."

"I do. I've had to relive that nightmare repeatedly at least once a month for the past 40 years."

"God he still looks young," I said sizing his face I had just mentally photographed against his age.

"That's what plastic surgery can do for you when half your skin gets melted off your face by napalm bomb dropped on a helicopter going into a hot LZ at Firebase Ranger."

"Bad timing?"

"No deliberate. The fast mover saw the chopper approaching the LZ and asked the Colonel for abort orders and the Colonel told the pilot no, proceed. I know this to be true because I talked to the pilot who dropped the bomb."

"That doesn't make sense," I said with anxiety flavoring my words.

"If you think about, if it makes a lot of sense if your career was riding on the amount of NVA KIAs you could net from this skirmish. You've got hundreds of NVA with their focus on shooting down this helicopter and not on the fast mover about to burning them alive into ashes.

"According to my sources, the helicopter was about 50 feet off the deck when the bomb went off below them. Since Robert could hear the radio chatter, he ordered everyone to close their doors and push up the windows.

"The chopper was completely engulfed in flames, crashed on its side and rolled away from all the napalm towards the friendly forces. Roberts co-pilot and door gunner were killed instantly. Robert got out."

"And saved both the crew chief and a second man from a fiery death despite having a broken leg, " I said with confidence like I knew the story by heart.

"Actually," she said, "He saved three. A gay Second Lieutenant by the name of Carmichael."

That took me a moment to digest. They I replied, "The Colonel's son was gay?"

"Robert decked Carmichael after he was awarded the Medal of Honor because Carmichael couldn't have the name tarnished by his gay son."

"Robert was a basket case when he got home both mentally and physically. I love him before and after, so I took him in. There were days when I wish I hadn't and days when his sunshine drenched my life.

"Do you know what a man in torment does? He tries killing himself with booze. The bottle never talks back. I learned to listen, put cold compresses on his head when he went into hot sweats. When he screamed in pain and agony, I soothe him with love and words of comfort.

"It has taken a long time, but he's learned to live with a limp and the sounds of the high-pitched screams only a dead man makes as he is burned alive. These are the memories Robert could have taken with him, but he won't."

A beeper goes off, she pulls it out of her purse and looks at it, upside down and backwards, I read the words, "Dr. Savannah Livingston, confirmed appointment for Private James Simmons at 10 a. m., your office.

She slipped her pager back into her purse.

"See that building across the street?"

"The one that looks burnt down?"

"There were 12 people on the third floor who were trapped by the flames and the fire department was too late to save.

"Robert saved all 12. That's my Robert. That's a real hero. Ready to be one when needed."

"You are coming back up?"

"Let me get another cigarette from you and I'll be right back up."

She handed me a cigarette and went back upstairs.

I focused my thoughts and my eyes on a man two streetlights away. Off in the distance was the lonely sound of a late-night freight train rumbling on steel through the sticky, muggy curtain of an ink black night.

I wondered now when he flipped the last of the cigarette out onto the street, how we build heroes for the moment. But they were always there and never go away.

And as he faded back into the ink of black air, I realized that heroes never fail at being amazing. Instead, we fail them by not being, as Dr. Savannah Livingston put it, "ready to be one when needed."

Walking up the stairs to her room, I thought to myself, this is going to be one hell of a story. One, only a hero would dare to write.

MAIL CALL

NEXT TO "IN COMING," "Mail Call" got the attention of the troops. While both found them crowding around each other, the later was reacting to the threat of death. The former was the mailroom clerk reacting to the threat of death.

I don't think a single man didn't expect his name to be called while letters started pouring out of the U.S. Mail mailbags.

I can't imagine what it would have been like if every piece of mail was addressed to the mailroom clerk and no one else.

Stars and Stripes:

The men of B Battery the 4th Battalion, 77th Aerial Field Artillery (AFA) acted like bulls in a china closet when they stuffed the mailroom clerk into a US Mail mailbag and stamped the bag with 'return to sender'.

Half frozen, the mailroom clerk was holding 20 pieces of mail. They were all addressed to him.

These same men then proceeded to blow the orderly room into smithereens and used the ashes to roasting marshmallows.

When the CO asked what happened and found out the mail was only for the mail clerk, he grabbed a stick and started roasting marshmallows with the rest of his men.

Guess they don't call it the Bull Pen for nothing.

My point is, the one thing you didn't do if you were a mail clerk is mess with the mail. Most never did.

There were also some other rules you learned but were never written. You never read over a soldier's shoulders, never asked to see his girls and never, ever laughed at a guy who got a Dear John letter.

Not everyone would go to mail call. The other 10% were so cherry – so new to being stationed in Nam – the mail hadn't caught up to them yet.

For some reason mail clerks were either very tall or very short. Most were shot. Why that was the case, I can't say. My guess is when the tunnel rats were going home the last 90 days had them doing the mail. Otherwise, I don't believe the height of a mailroom clerk was legal.

These guys were so small they made short timer – a combat hat on pair of jungle boots – look tall.

Okay, maybe not that small but I'm willing to bet the guy doing the mail had wished he was that small on days when one or two pieces of mail came in for himself and no one else.

And when Kentucky didn't get any mail, you didn't have to be in the same building with him to know he was going off on the poor mail clerk.

"Whhaat you mean their ain't no way no mail for me, boy, I'm going to kick youur aaasss," he would wail. The men got a good laugh out of that and headed for the mess hall.

Mail Clerks also had to deal with something even more insidious than the female snake in an envelope. In fact, this kind of snake was a real, cold blooded and had fangs. So, placing one's hand into a seemingly empty mailbag could be hazardous to one's health.

Too, these mailroom guys, I swear, were from a different planet. Or at least a different country. English was a second language and they were proud of that fact, too.

Four very specific kinds of mail came out of those mailbags. Letters from moms, care packages from moms, letters from future moms, and mental letter bombs fused by dear Johns.

The rest was men's magazines and pure, cheap and

rude sex scandals made shows like MASH look like a baby in diapers. The kind of stuff that the tabloids cringe trying to report on.

Most of that material headed for the out houses where a little more than pee and feces was being deposited in the shittier.

I harbor the belief that spamming became an art form way before the birth of Christ. A system of making money from someone else's ledger only got better over time.

As soon as you come to realize that major magazines were selling their mailing addresses to a wide variety of companies throughout the world, the easier it will be for you to realize that soldiers in Vietnam were not only hot property for the US military.

They were also lucrative gold mines for what we now call spam. Only, it was sexual and filthy.

I'm all for a good dose of sexy and filthy.

And from this where on girl could talk to hundreds of guys per week, the better you are at understanding where $2,500,000 per month was going.

The first letter was an introduction. If the soldier responded back, images of a girl were sent with a tease letter which said, basically, send me $50 and all show you all of me. Then came the strip show followed up with $100 will get you some pink. It wasn't that straight on. But that's the jest of it.

Playboy was cheaper.

Then there were the supposedly "legitimate girls" but they were after the $40,000.

These black widows would fly to Japan or Australia, get hitched, make sure the guy was the type that would go nuts with a dear John letter and send him a picture of herself being sexed up by another guy and then tell the soldier goodbye.

Of course, the reverse was true, the guys knew how

to play the women the same way. Assuming they were chatting to real women. I knew of three married guys with 12 girls writing to him once a week.

Personally, I liked the TasteyKakes my mom sent me. The Butter Scotch ones hit the spot. That plus the homemade fudge brought home to my Vietnam cot. I lived for these once a month care packages.

Scented letters made the hooch smell better than the smell of men, brasso, and weapon cleaning fluid.

I don't know if that was a new thing for the Vietnam conflict or not, but those perfumed letters sure smelled good. Only thing better would have been the physical presence of the soft, warm skin wearing it up close and personal.

When a quiet one got a Dear John, we all went on 24-hour alert.

It was the quiet one that would take you with him if he decided to go.

ICE CREAM TRUCKS WEAPONS OF MASS DESTRUCTION

I'LL SAY IT ONCE and I'll say it again and again, it was the little things that made the fondest memories for me. Consider Ice cream one of those things that made the summertime miserable in Vietnam. Short of a deep drought of it there, the second most demoralizing item on the list was the lack of Coco-Cola.

I also harbor the belief; if the NVA soldiers were fed the food we were fed in Vietnam that they would have completely surrendered unconditionally. Hell, we didn't even have a Starbucks on every corner much less a Good Humor Ice Cream truck.

You can pretty much imagine my horror when I was told the Good Humor Ice Cream man – along with his truck – was nowhere to be found. I wanted to start a Good Humor Ice Cream petition and send it to all the members of congress as soon as I heard about that!

Can you imagine a world without Ice Cream? Why it was cruel and unusual punishment, let me tell you! Someone needed to make it a war crime!

Dear Mr. President,

I don't expect a combat zone to have all the creature comforts of home and when I signed up I knew some of the benefits of being in a combat zone did not include American women, big named concerts, strippers, steak or sufficient amounts of cold soda pop.

But cutting my supply line to Ice Cream, well, that's not going to cut it, I quit.

Thank you, Sir.

PS. Where's my Starbucks? (Editors note: The writer must have been high when he wrote this, there was no Starbucks yet.)

Of course, once you sign on the dotted line, you come to realize the word choice has been stricken from the words used in the US Army vocabulary. Still, if I had a choice between steak and American women, I'd go for the steak hands down.

I think they were trying to keep us lean and mean with some of the stuff that was either not available or are temporarily out of stock. And temporarily out of stock meant, if it was seasonal and in demand, it wasn't going to be stocked locally until it was out of season.

I harbor the belief that if we were able to SYOPS Ice Cream, for certain, the outcome of our war efforts in Vietnam would have been completely different.

NEW MOBILE WEAPONS OF MASS DISTRUCTION

I DID FIND OUT that the military was seriously considering the following to vehicle prototypes as candidates for deployment in South Vietnam.

This one was removed from the list due to its high center of gravity. While it turned out that the designed truly confused the enemy it was unable to see much less shoot the one million nitrogen cooled star shaped ice cream sandwiches.

The Army planned on using them along the Hồ Chí Minh trail until they realized the cost of supplying these vehicles with the sandwiches – code name: cold cream – far exceeded the number of enemy soldiers.

It was rumored that half the supply disappeared after entering Vietnam.

This vehicle was considered as a multi-purpose command center. Looking much like an UH-1H Huey –pregnant with twins – without rotor blades, its true purpose was to spurt mustard and ketchup out from the back end while playing the Star-Spangled Banner.

While unclear how those two had any SYOPS relevance or value, SYOPS insisted that the nap on strikes right after dousing the enemy with spurts mustard and ketchup would put new meaning into the phrase "well done".

Sigh, a little color to an otherwise Olive Drab world.

You would think that this delicious cold product

would be a big hit with the men.

It wasn't available.

Why?

For a couple of reasons.

One, Ice cream requires refrigeration and that takes fuel and electricity.

Very few of the temporary quarters had electricity and the ones that did would not have enough voltage to maintain the use of a private refrigerator for each soldier in the hooch.

Even if you could have one refrigerator in each hooch – which a few did – there are additional issues with having one. Aside from brown outs or black outs, there are some serious risks with owning a rather large refrigerator,

Consider the following refrigerator scenarios and, please, don't try these at home.

THE NARC ELIMINATOR

This is where you get the narcotics agent drunk and shove him inside.

THE SINGAPORE SLAMMER

This is where you get the NCO drunk and shove him inside.

THE SIBERIAN EXPRESS

This is where you get the REFER drunk and shove him inside.

THE DOPE A REEFER

This is where you harvest Mary Jane and grow it inside.

THE JEFFERSON SKY ROCKET EXPRESS

Okay, this one is a long shot. Place the Hooch Jack Ass into a refrigerator. Secure the sides of the unit with ample enough rockets for primary and secondary lift the way the US with a degree in rocket science said to do it. And fire off the rockets.

While it is feasibly doable, there are some other

CONSIDERATIONS one might want to look at.

The first of which – a minor annoyance – is gravity. PSST. There's warheads on those rockets. I'm sure the hooch Jack Ass hadn't thought of that.

The second, really annoying over looked detail is the fact that the rockets spin. No biggie, since the human parcel has probably been G forced into non-existence by the time his body filled the refer with V8 juice!

The third, assuming the first two didn't kill him involves a – it is rather trivial, really – oxygen.

That combined with another not important fact is it is cold at 10,000 feet. Assuming a parachute egress at 10,000 feet and, without the proper clothing, the hooch Jack Ass would either die from asphyxiation or hypothermia.

But let's assume he managed to survive all the above, used a paraglider chute and was smart enough to build an engine driven prop he strapped on his back. He could wind up in Laos, North Vietnam, South Vietnam or in the China Sea.

Not one of those locations would be far enough away to not be facing some hard times.

So, if our hooch Jack Ass did manage to pull it off, he would most likely find himself in a worse situation.

But the guys left behind have some serious problems to deal with. How are you going to explain the hole in the roof of the hooch? Or the missing rockets? Or our missing hooch Jack Ass?

Besides, this one was done once before by a China Empire around 4000 BC – might want to ask him how it worked out for him.

Okay, none of this ever happened. I call this human muse. If we couldn't laugh at ourselves or come up with these zany ideas, what would life be worth living for?

As for creativity, the stuff that work was called field expediency.

Richard T. Edwards

YOU HAD TO DIE TO GET BETTER

FRANK OZ WOKE UP, shot his alarm clock with a finger gun and hit the floor.

Around him was chaos. A private war around him told of organized promises that were never finished. A jungle war of unopened bills, letters of rejection and unread newspapers he would use, someday, for a fireplace that hadn't been used for 30 years.

The smell of old trash, cigars and his best of buddies, the coffee machine filling the one bedroom with the aroma of Starbucks Sumatra.

The day had been already up past the rush hour traffic. He stretched his 6-foot frame, revealing the scar that won him a purple heart. Heard his dead wife's voice tell him as he scanned the room for the dark green pack of Kools, "finish it for me."

The room felt colder with that memory. "I will. Today," he thought as he headed for the shower with a slight hint of a tear welling in his eyes. It wasn't fair, he thought, she left the world first. And me alone.

He had three hours to cook up a hook for his book and all he could think about was his stomach which ached from three-day old pizza and the six-pack of beer. Resolution came in the form of two slices of bacon, one sunny side up egg and two pieces of toast.

He smiled to himself over that thought, dried off the body and the three-year-old beard, didn't confront the man in the mirror and walked naked into the kitchen.

His cell phone rang. He already knew who it was.

"You know, they should give you a medal for

relentless, Carmon."

"Frank," started Carmon, "Just tell me the revisions will be in my e-mail by one."

"Alright, the revisions will be there by Two." And with that, he hung up on her.

The bacon was about to burn and the popping grease firing molecular-level buckshots at his skin let him know two things. One the pan was too hot and, two, cooking naked can be hazardous to one's health.

He shouted a lot of obscenities and made a mental note to never do that again. And then wondered how hairless apes as a species survived cooking meat over a wood fire. Guess, he mused, a few would have to die to teach the experience to the living, so they wouldn't do the same and die.

A smile grew on Franks face. As he realized he had the hook he was looking for. He wrote it down on a piece of paper and then ate breakfast. After that, he cleaned up his apartment. Something that hadn't been done in almost three years.

At 1:45 pm, he put the hook right where it was needed and then sent the finished chapter over to Carmen.

Who promptly called Frank.

"Oh, my god, Frank. That's brilliant!" remarked Carmon.

"It had to be," replied Frank.

The line was quite simple and to the point.

"You had to die to get better."

Thank you for reading.
Please review this book. Reviews help others find Absolutely Amazing eBooks and inspire us to keep providing these marvelous tales.

If you would like to be put on our email list to receive updates on new releases, contests, and promotions, please go to AbsolutelyAmazingEbooks.com and sign up.

ABOUT THE AUTHOR

Richard T. Edwards's life has been full of some pretty amazing people places and things. As a seasoned writer and photographer for the past 50 years he has had over 2,000 bylines. His best memories are the times he was in the service. Especially, his time in Vietnam.

Richard T. Edwards

The New Atlantian Library

NewAtlantianLibrary.com
or AbsolutelyAmazingeBooks.com
or AA-eBooks.com

www.ingramcontent.com/pod-product-compliance
Lightning Source LLC
Chambersburg PA
CBHW070536170426
43200CB00011B/2443